Fountain Wells

Fountain Wells

Oilfield Novels of
Ontario, Pennsylvania,
Ohio, and West Virginia

Dick Heaberlin

A Cavalcade of Oilfield Novels

Orange House Book
San Marcos, Texas

For additional information visit the author's website at DickHeaberlinWrites.com.

Copyright 2008 by Dick Heaberlin

ISBN 978-0-9794964-4-8

For Andrea

Contents

A Cavalcade of Oilfield Novels	8
Chapter 1 Skimming and Drilling	17
Chapter 2 The First Oilfield Novel	21
Chapter 3 Petrolia: Site Of the Early Oilfield Novels	28
Chapter 4 Booming and Blasting	35
Chapter 5 More Blasting	48
Chapter 6 Two Short Stories	58
Chapter 7 A Young Englishman In the Oilfield	65
Chapter 8 Rockefeller and the Standard	73
Chapter 9 Monopoly	82

Chapter 10
An Early Ohio Oilfield Novel   85

Chapter 11
Refining Rivals   89

Chapter 12
In Defense of Standard   93

Chapter 13
Shooter Shot   101

Chapter 14
Law and Oil   106

Chapter 15
Oil and a Church in West Virginia   121

Chapter 16
Gauging and Scouting   127

Chapter 17
Novels of the 1940s and 1950s   158

Chapter 18
Golden Butterfly   174

Works Cited   176

Index   179

A Cavalcade of Oilfield Novels

It's shoulder season 2008, and the Azaleas are blooming. So are oil prices. A barrel of oil has recently sold for over $113 dollars a barrel. The pundits on CNBC and Bloomberg tell us why. It's speculation. Maybe it is. But maybe we have reached peak oil. That's the question. How much is left down there? Can we get it out? How much will it cost? As world demand soars, can we be saved by LNG, coal to oil, oil sands? What are the environmental effects of these sources. The questions come easier than the answers. Knowledge and technology, can they save us?

Some people seek the answer to these and other questions in reading histories of the oil industry. I don't really expect answers there, but I know from reading these histories that from the earliest times, the seekers of oil were as uncertain as we are. From day to day with each new discovery they would go from oil scarcity to oil glut. I like reading these histories, particularly the illustrated ones. But I like even more reading the novels about the oilfields, about the dangers and difficulties of getting the oil out and to the buyer.

When I took a course in the English novel in college, I discovered a wonderful resource: Edward Wagenknecht's *Cavalcade of the English Novel*. From reading it, I was able to put the novels I read in context of other works written at the same time, many of which were rare and unavailable to me. I hope with these books to provide a similar service. Many of the oilfield novels I survey in these volumes are rare. I am able to provide this survey only because I have been persistent in finding these books on internet sites such as Abe Books, Alibris, and Amazon. I also have had available to me the remarkable collection of the Perry Castaneda library at the University of Texas in Austin.

In *A Cavalcade*, I describe and discuss the important novels written about the oilfield from the first one in 1876 to those of the present. I've arranged the material chronologically within the area of the oilfields, beginning with the earliest oilfields in the east. Most of the early novels are set along the wooded creeks and hills of Western Pennsylvania, a land of small farmers and lumbermen. I've followed the movement of the oilfields west to Texas. Then I've moved to the Blackjack-Oak lands of Oklahoma, moving from there to the Western States. It's quite a tour. I want to make readers aware of a relatively unknown segment of our literary history. I rarely provide literary criticism, for readers may have little interest in it until they know of these works and have an opportunity to read them. I focus more on the scenes in the oilfield and less on the financial dealings and lives and loves of the oil poor and oil wealthy.

From Wildcat to Ghost Town

I have arranged the cavalcade to emphasize the differences place has on oilfield fiction, but there is an amazing similarity from place to place. Typically a wildcatter has an idea that there is oil under the ground in some new place. He may have decided this by using a divining rod, by observing oil seeps, by using some concept about salt domes, or by employing the latest in seismological surveying. In any case, he must drill to get the oil, so he must raise the capital to pay for the leases and drilling. Sometimes, he is spending what he made on his last discovery. Sometimes, he is finding backers, perhaps local people eager for the wealth that comes with oil.

Then he must get the leases allowing him to drill. How easy or expensive this is depends on the competition and his likelihood of drilling success. If he is close to another oilfield and the major companies are bidding against him, he may have to pay a large fee as bonus to get the lease and pay a larger share of the oil. He will want to secure a large acreage and not have to worry about competition once he has completed the well. But he may have to settle for a lease on a drilling site as small as the backyard of a house.

Once he gets the lease and backing, he must select a drilling site on his lease, hire his crew, buy a drilling rig, get it to the site, and build or have built a derrick. Any and all of these steps can be extremely difficult depending on the circumstances, particularly distance from other drilling activity, availability of transportation, and the nature of the site. A wildcatter drilling in a swamp far from a railroad with no oil activity nearby may have little chance of drilling successfully. If there is much or no drilling nearby, he may have difficulty finding a competent drilling crew. A crew is usually supervised by a foreman, called a tool pusher, and led by a driller, who makes the crucial decisions about how to drill the hole. At different times, the duties and terms for the crew varied. There were roustabouts, roughnecks, and derrick men. On cable tool rigs, there was a tool dresser who kept the drill bits sharp. Workers on cable tool rigs were called *jarheads,* and those on rotary rigs *swivelnecks.*

Once all the preparation work has been done, the crew spuds in (initial drilling with a large bit) and begins drilling. Thousands of things can go wrong. The bit can be stuck in the hole, twisted off, or dulled by hard rock. Pockets of gas can throw the drill stem from the well. Boilers can explode. The cables can break. Crews can be injured, get sick, be poisoned by gas, be highjacked, get drunk, or quit. The derrick can be blown over by a storm or burned. The site can be flooded or attacked by hijackers.

If all these adversities are overcome, the well still can be dry, or apparently so. The wildcatter has to decide when to give up and cut his losses. If the well has oil, it may not be of sufficient quantity or quality to justify development. Or the small amount of oil found may not justify the expense of transporting it to a distant railhead or refinery. If the flow of oil is small, the well may be exploded with nitroglycerin shells in hopes of increasing the yield.

If the well flows or can be pumped profitably, the wildcatter must provide storage for the oil and make arrangements to transport and sell it. He must also drill other wells to prove up his lease. He must arrange financing for all these, sometimes forcing him to sell all or part of his holding in the well or lease.

If the discovery is sufficiently large, very soon others are drilling on nearby leases. Sometimes, leases are drilled so compactly that one can step from derrick to derrick without reaching ground. There is increasing danger of fire as new gushers come in. Sometimes, gas and oil gushes from a nearby well and catches fire causing stored oil and neighboring wells to burn. It may take days or weeks to be put out. Putting out fires is very expensive and often leads to the financial failure of the developer.

Many wildcatters choose to sell out once they have found oil. Some sell because they never know how long the oil will last, and they choose to take the sure thing. Others sell so that they can go on to the next wildcat territory—because they think drilling and developing a field a dull business.

To develop a large field requires many people doing many different things. The unemployed rush to the field to find jobs as teamsters, store clerks, carpenters, pipeline workers, cooks, waitresses, derrick builders, lease hounds, lawyers. Some of the less savory come from other boom towns. There are bootleggers, prostitutes, gamblers, extortionists, hijackers, and swindlers. All of these come in great numbers. Housing is expensive and poor. Often the wells are soon pumped out, and the whole motley crew moves to the next discovery field.

Why They Write Oilfield Novels

Some of those who left the oilfield went on to become writers, telling of their and their family's experience during those exciting times. Oilfield novels are about people — what they do, what they want, think, feel, care about, what they are capable of — their endurance, hardiness, courage. Oilfield novels are about people in conflict, striving to get what they want, using whatever skills and knowledge they have to do what they must do. There is an intensity to life in an oilfield lacking in most places. The stakes are high. Characters in oilfield novels reveal their strengths and weaknesses — good and evil — more readily because of this intensity.

Novels set in oilfields are by nature historical. They are about particular oilfields developed by particular people. Most of the authors of the novels have had first-hand experience in the field either as participants, family members, or observers. Some of the novels provide excellent historical information about the occurrences in particular fields. Others are remarkably fanciful, full of historical inaccuracies.

Historians and novelists have shown us how dangerous oilfields are. Novelists have been able to dramatize it more, make us care about the fate of the characters we have come to know. The activity in and around oilfields provided rich grist for the novelists' mills. They particularly have liked the suddenness of events in an oilfield — with people growing rich rapidly and broke as quickly.

The novelists have liked also the apparent randomness of it — how one would drill and the oil would come gushing out and how another would drill and drill and drill and get nothing, just dust. They've liked its danger — how oil workers could be gassed, burned, caught in the machinery, or blown to bits by nitroglycerin. They've liked showing the courage with which the workers faced these dangers and their hardiness and stoicism as they faced difficult working conditions — extreme cold, long hours, heavy physical labor. They've liked the friendships that came through shared labor, liked the willingness of people to suffer for others, to face danger to save their friends. They've liked showing soft, ambitious young men maturing as they faced these hardships, liked showing them becoming more physically fit, more technically proficient, liked showing people moving up from toolie to driller to producer, liked showing the newly rich young man marrying the aristocratic girl, going from frog to prince with his princess. They've liked explaining how the equipment worked, for example describing in detail the working of the cable tool rig, its bullwheel and calfwheel. They've liked talking about the changes that came over people because of the sudden wealth, liked describing the excesses of people such as Coal Oil Johnny, legendary big spender. They've liked describing the boomtown, with all the hangers-on — the bootleggers, the prostitutes, the robbers, the gamblers, liked the irony of the good-hearted honest madam. They've liked the conmen and their schemes for quick riches, and they've liked seeing the conmen getting their just deserts, particularly when their punishment comes at the hands of the hard-working young hero. They've liked showing the other kinds of villains — the bullies, whether those using finances or fist. Some concerned themselves with social evils — for example, the pollution caused by the oil or the mistreatment of the workers, particularly old workers.

The experiences of workers and boomers in one oilfield have not been the same as in another. There have been different kinds of people owning the land, different laws governing the drilling and ownership, different kinds and degrees of law enforcement in effect, different working conditions prevailing, different machinery and resources available to the driller. It all leads to a wonderful mix, novels of excitement. Few novelists are able to resist describing a sensational oil-well fire or explosion. Few can pass up describing the crowded excitement of the boomtown—its lawlessness, its squalor, its excess.

The Cavalcade begins in Ontario and Western Pennsylvania in the 1850s.

Illustrations

Cover images is taken from the cover of *"646" and the Trouble Man*

Map of Petrolia from George Lindstrom's *Out of the Sand*.   29

Cover image of *The Devil's Hat*.   34

Dusty and Phin pole to safety in *Prince Dusty*.   51

Gas and water come before the oil in *Prince Dusty*   57

Cover image of *The Wild-Catters*.   64

George scouts for Staines in *The Wild-Catters*   66

Cover image of *The Spotter*   102

"Here ole man, I'll gin it to you first." from *Tract Number 3377*.   108

"It was laughable to see poor Jennings trying to protect his trees." from *Tract Number 3377*   115

"Yer Mystery's eout tekin' the' mornin' air, eh?" from *Tract Number 3377* 117

"Burning tanks of oil boiled over." from *Tract Number 3377*.   119

Cover image from *The Church on Quintuple Mountain*   122

"I don't think I'm hurt, he said, feeling his feet and leg." from *"646" and the Trouble Man*.   143

Chapter 1

Skimming and Drilling

These days with oil over $100 a barrel, we do lots of talking about oil, but that's nothing new. From ancient times oil has been noted and discussed. Accounts of oil in the new world appeared in the reports of many early-day explorers. But oil had no place in fiction until it could be important enough economically to bring masses of people into the oilfield. As long as it was limited to the quantities that could be gathered by skimming from oil seeps such as those in the Allegheny region northwest of Pittsburgh, oil would remain mainly a nuisance.

Oil first came in an economically worthwhile quantity as a result of techniques developed for drilling for salt brine. In the early nineteenth century, salt was a valuable commodity, so in Kentucky, where there were many salt domes, water-well drillers were hired to bring up the salt brine. The Ruffner brothers, David and Joseph, developed an improved process in order to reach the brine. They began drilling near Charleston, West Virginia, in 1806, and finished in 1808, having drilled to a depth of fifty-eight feet. The techniques they developed were improved upon, and by 1854 a rig had drilled a 2193-ft well. Among the innovations were using copper tubing for casing, using "jars" or "slips" in the drill stem, and filling the space between the tubing and the rock with seed bags.

(History of Oil Well Drilling 71)

After the Ruffner brothers drilled their first well, many drillers of water wells or brine wells, using improved versions of their techniques, discovered gas and oil instead of brine. At first, the oil was considered an inconvenience and allowed to run into rivers and creeks. *(The American Petroleum Industry 17)* But in the late 1830's The American Medical Oil Company was organized in Burkeville, Kentucky, to market the oil running into the Cumberland River from a salt well, reportedly thousands of barrels. The company continued to market oil as a medicine over the following years selling thousands of bottles in the U. S. and Europe. *(API 17)*

But it was another salt well that led to the first well drilled with the intent of finding oil. In 1839, in Tarentum, Pennsylvania, Thomas Kier and his son, Samuel, hired a veteran water-well driller to drill a salt well for them. At 465 feet he struck salt water but with it small quantities of petroleum. At first the Kiers and a neighbor who had a similar well just drained the oil and dumped it into the Pennsylvania canal. When Samuel Kier's wife became ill, he noticed that the "American Oil" prescribed for his wife was similar to the oil he was throwing away. He remembered that in his local area, Seneca oil had been used as a medicine. He leased his neighbor's well and began bottling and selling the oil in Pittsburgh as a medicine. In 1850, Samuel Kier began refining his excess oil in a one-gallon still, thus becoming America's first refiner of petroleum. *(EDO 3)* Kier's success was mostly due to his skill in advertising. In one of his advertisements, he wrote that the oil was a by-product of a salt well. Supposedly, George Bissell saw this advertisement, and it gave him the idea which led three years later to the first drilling of an oil well. Williamson and Daum doubt this story, but they admit that Bissell knew of oil being taken from salt wells. *(API 18-22)*

Bissell was a leader in setting up the company that was responsible for drilling the first oil well. For several years. Bissell and Francis Brewer worked with bankers in Connecticut in establishing an oil company. James Townsend was the leading banker in setting up Seneca Oil of Connecticut in March of 1858, and he hired Edwin L. Drake, a railroad conductor, who, having fallen ill, had to give up his work on the railroad. He had no qualifications apparently for leading the operation, but he was available and had a rail pass which enabled him to ride free to Titusville on Oil Creek, the site they had picked for their attempt. He arrived in Titusville with the new title, Colonel, and a stove-pipe hat. Drake spent months looking for someone with experience to drill the well. Finally he found William A., "Uncle Billy," Smith, a blacksmith from Tarentum to drill it. Uncle Billy brought his family to Titusville in mid May after having built much of the equipment they would need in his shop in Tarentum. The investors became very cautious of wasting their money, and after spending $2,000 by April, they provided Drake only $847 to finish the job. James Townsend provided some funds, but by late in August even he stopped contributing. Townsend sent Drake a final remittance which was to pay off the obligations, and Townsend instructed him to abandon the well. Uncle Billy Smith lived at the well, and on Sunday August 28th the crew had pulled the tools from the well after reaching 69' 6". Smith looked into the pipe and thought he saw a film on the water. He plugged the end of a piece of rain spout and put it into the well. He pulled it out and saw that he had oil, having completed the first oil well in the U. S. Drake rigged a hand pump and twenty foot piece of pipe, joining the handle with a walking beam, and the well was on pump, producing eight to ten gallons a day. Within a few days the check from Townsend with the instruction to close down arrived. (*API* 72-81)

Chapter 2

The First Oilfield Novel

Surprisingly, the first oil novel was not about Pennsylvania, nor was it written by an American, nor published in America. It was set in Canada and based on the discovery of Canadian Hugh Nixon Shaw. Shaw owned only one acre and had almost no money but managed to drill a gusher on January 16, 1862, in Oil Springs, Ontario. (www.rvtravelog.com/canada.dir/canadaoil.dir/canadaoil1.htm) Based on Hugh Nixon Shaw's discovery, Walter Besant and James Rice, two English novelists, published the first novel concerning the oil business, *The Golden Butterfly* in 1876. It is mainly a novel of manners and romance, but one of the many pivotal figures in the story is Gilead P. Beck, an American. Though the story takes place mostly in London, it begins with a prologue set in the foothills of the Sierra Madres shortly after the gold rush. Two English travelers—Tommy Ladds, Captain of the 35th Dragoons, and his young friend, Roland "Jack" Dunquerque—see a man being chased by a bear. After watching the event for a while, they decide to shoot the bear. Thus, they rescue and then meet Gilead P. Beck. Beck is an impoverished but upper middle-class seeker after gold. But all he has managed to acquire is a golden butterfly, a charm given him by a "squaw" he has befriended. He has been told that as long as the butterfly remains unbroken, his luck will continue. Beck is aided by his new friends and provided with new clothes and a railway ticket to New York.

Chapter One and several subsequent chapters set in London introduce other important characters, all revealing something of the manners of the London of the time. We meet the young heroine, bright and well-read and interesting, Phillis Fleming. We meet Gabriel Cassillis, a wealthy friend of these folks and of Ladds, and Dunquerque. At a party at the Cassillis, Jack meets Phillis and ultimately they find their way to love. Surprisingly, also at the party is Gilead P. Beck, now richer than rich.

Beck tells them of how he has fared after he left them. He went to New York City, but he says he left it because it is not a city for the poor. From there he moved to the city of Limerick on Lake Ontario. He worked doing chores for the "delooded" farmers there. They thought he was crazy, but he explains his purpose:

> They thought too that I was mad when I began to buy the land. You could buy it for nothing; a dollar an acre; half a dollar an acre; anything an acre. I've mended a cart-wheel for a five-acre lot of swamp. They laughed at me. The children used to cry out when I passed along, 'There goes mad Beck." But I bought all I could, and my only regret was that I couldn't buy up the hull township — clear off men, women, and children, and start fresh. (*Golden Butterfly* 107)

Then his friends ask him about what the golden butterfly was doing all this time. He says that it was around his neck and that it was "whisperin' and eggin' me on because it was bound to fulfill the old squaw's prophecy." (*GB* 108) He told about the land he bought:

> I saw, sir, a barren bog. If it had been a land as fertile as the land of Canaan, that would not have made my heart to bound as it did bound when I looked across that swamp; for I never was a tiller or a lover of the soil. A barren bog it was. The barrenest, boggiest part of it all was my claim; when the natives spoke of it they called it Beck's Farm, and then the poor critturs squirmed in their chairs and laughed. Yes, they laughed. Beck's Farm, they said. It was the only thing they had to laugh about. Wall, up and down the face of that almighty bog there ran creeks, and after rainy weather the water stood about on the morasses. Plenty of water, but a curious thing, none of it fit to drink. No living thing except man would set his lips to that brackish, bad-smelling water. And that wasn't all; sometimes a thick black slime rose to the surface of the marsh and lay there an inch thick, sometimes you came upon patches of 'gum-beds,' as they called them, where the ground was like tar, and smelt strong. That is what I saw when I looked around, sir. And to think that those poor mean pork raisers saw it all the same as I did and never suspected! Only cursed the gifts of the Lord when they weren't laughing at Beck's Farm. (*GB* 111)

His former acquaintances think he has struck gold. He corrects them:

> "Ile. Gold you have to dig, to pick, to wash. Gold means rheumatism and a bent back. Ile flows, and you become suddenly rich. You make all the loafers around fill your pails for you. And then your bankers tell you how many millions of dollars you are worth."

"Millions!" repeated Jack. " The word sounds very rich and luxurious."

"It is so, sir. There's nothing like it in the Old Country. England is a beautiful place, and London is a beautiful city. You've got many blessin's in this beautiful city.... But one thing this country has not got, and that is — Ile.

"It is nearly a year since I made up my mind to begin my well. I knew it was there, because I'd been in Pennsylvania and learned the signs; it was only the question whether I should strike it, and where. The neighbours thought I was digging for water, and figured around with their superior intellecks, because they were certain the water would be brackish. Then they got tired of watching, and I worked on. Boring a well is not quite the sort of work a man would select for a pleasant and variegated occupation. I reckon it's monotonous; but I worked on. I knew what was coming; I thought o' that Indian squaw; and I always had my Golden Butterfly tied in a box at my back. I bored and I bored. Day after day I bored. In that lonely miasmatic bog I bored all day and best part of the night. For nothing came, and sometimes qualms crossed my mind that perhaps there would never be anything. But always there was the gummy mud, smelling of what I knew was below, to lead me on.

"It was the ninth day, and noon. I had a shanty called the farmhouse, about a hundred yards from my well. And there I was taking my dinner." (*GB* 108)

His friends asked him if the golden butterfly went down into the well, and he said that nothing went down. Then he told of the first gusher recorded in fiction:

"But something came up—up like a fountain, up like the bubbling over of the airth's eternal teapot; a black muddy jet of stuff. Great sun! I think I see it now."

He paused and sighed.

"It was nearly all Ile, pure and unadulterated, from the world's workshop. Would you believe it, gentlemen? There were not enough bar'ls, not by hundreds, in the neighbourhood all round Limerick City, to catch that Ile. It flowed in a stream three feet down the creek; it was carried away into the lake and lost; it ran free and uninterrupted for three days and three nights. We saved what we could. The neighbours brought their pails, their buckets, their basins, their kettles; there was not a utensil of any kind that was not filled with Ile, from the pig's trough to the child's pap-bowl. Not one. It ran and it ran. When the first flow subsided we calculated that seven million bar'ls had been wasted and lost. Seven millions! I am a Christian man, and grateful to the Butterfly, but I sometimes repine when I think of that wasted Ile. Every bar'l worth nine dollars at least, and most likely ten. Sixty-three millions of dollars. Twelve millions of pounds sterling lost in three days for want of a few coopers...."

"The great spurt subsided, and we went to work in earnest. That well has continued to yield five hundred bar'ls daily. That is four thousand five hundred dollars in my pocket every four and twenty hours."
(*GB* 111)

This explanation isn't too far from what happened in Oil Springs, Ontario. Much oil was wasted, but hardly the seven million barrels described here. The well in Canada didn't subside. A means was discovered for capping it, one using a leather bag and flax seed.(http://www.science.uwaterloo.ca/earth/waton/s937.html) He goes on to describe some of the results of his discovery:

> There are wells of mine sunk all over the place; the swamp is covered with Gilead P. Beck's derricks. The township of Limerick has become the city of Rockoleaville—my name, that was—and a virtuous and industrious population are all engaged morning, noon, and night in fillin' my pails. There's twenty-five bars, I believe, at this moment. There are three meetin'-houses and two daily papers, and there air fifteen lawyers. (*GB* 111-2)

Brief as it is, this is the first description of an oil boomtown in fiction.

Gilead P. Beck is rich and has come to London because he believes he will be better accepted there than he would be as the newly rich oil man in New York. He remains there and socializes with such rich, important people as Gabriel Cassillis. Unfortunately, Beck allows Cassillis to invest all of his money, and Cassillis loses all of it and all of his own by investing in a worthless stock—Eldorado. Simultaneously, Beck gets word that his wells have run dry and that his bank account is empty. He looks in his box and discovers that the golden butterfly is broken. But he takes his loss without fretting. When he hears of Phillis Fleming's betrothal to Jack Dunquerque, he gives the golden insect to her. She and Jack are planning to move to Virginia to begin a new life. Beck persuades Mrs. Agatha L'Estrange to marry him, and they also decide to move to Virginia to start over. He sells some art works, all that he had remaining of his oil wealth. She still has some money, so they will get by but never be rich again.

We find them in the final chapter happy in love:

> On a verandah in sunny Virginia, Agatha Beck sits quietly working, and crooning some old song in sheer content and peace of heart. Presently she lifts her head as she hears a step. That smile with which she greets her husband shows that she is happy in her new life." (*GB* 543)

Gilead informs her that Jack and Phillis and their new baby are coming. Once they arrive, Phillis surprises Gilead by showing him the baby with the golden butterfly around his neck. Beck is surprised:

> "That Inseck!" said Gilead sentimentally. "Wal, it's given me the best thing that a man can get" — he took the hand of his wife — "love and friendship. You are welcome, Phillis, to all the rest, provided that all the rest does not take away these."
>
> "Nay," she said, her eyes filling with the gentle dew of happiness and content; "I have all that I want for myself. I have my husband and my boy — my little, little Philip! I am more than happy; and so I give to tiny Phil all the remaining Luck of the Golden Butterfly." (*GB* 543)

And with those words, the first oil novel ends. In it, love and happiness are more important than the wealth brought by the discovery and production of oil.

Chapter 3

Petrolia: Site Of the Early Oilfield Novels

Titusville the site of the first oil well in Pennsylvania, is on Oil Creek just a few miles above where the creek runs into the Allegheny River. At the time, most people thought oil could only be found along creeks where oil seeped. Soon, the entire creek was leased and lined with wells and refineries. Even from the earliest days, many of the wells were found to be dry. These were simply abandoned with no effort to clean them up. Soon the hillsides had been stripped of their timber. A good book describing the early-day excesses and environmental degradation is Brian Black's *Petrolia: The Landscape of America's First Oil Boom*. That is an apt title because the valley of oil creek came to be called Petrolia. And the area boomed, boomed, and boomed.

People came from all over the world to participate. Newspapers sent their reporters, who enthusiastically endorsed what they saw. Investors rushed in to spend their money. A few became almost instantly rich. Many lost what they had. Some grew rich, lost what they had, and grew rich again. The early oil producers were seldom college graduates. The largest group of oil workers came from those who had been in the local lumbering business. Salt drillers came to the area,

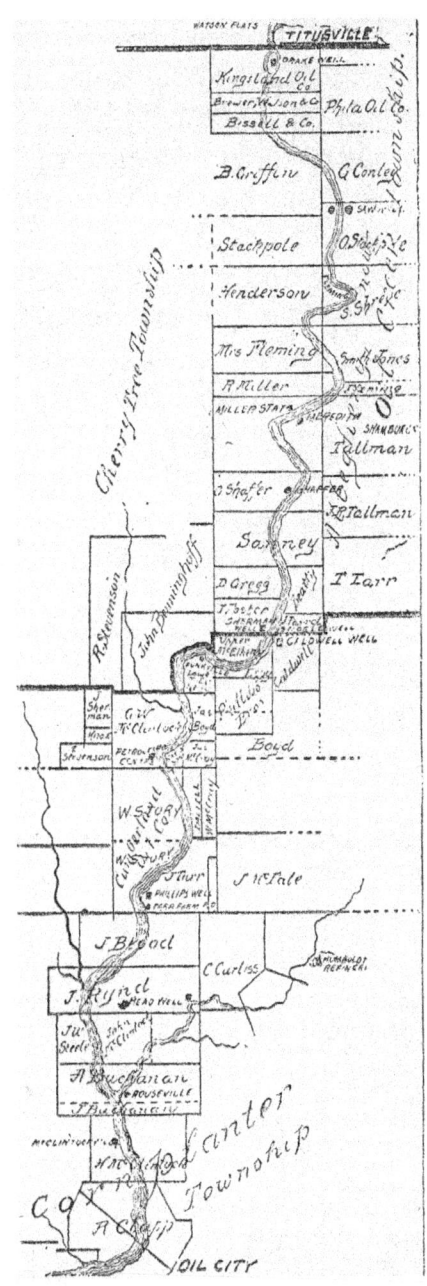

Map of Petrolia from George Lindstrom's *Out of the Sand*.

began by drilling, and often became producers and owners. Local farmers grew wealthy from royalty payments, but few got into producing. Many of the early producers had been clerks in mercantile operations. All ages of people came, but they were most frequently in their thirties and forties. (API 88-89)

The rush to lease and pump was even more frenzied than in mining boom towns, for unlike gold and silver, oil was fugacious — moving under ground. If you didn't pump the oil from under your land, your neighbor would. Each person's rushing to get his oil led to overproduction, with wells being drilled with derricks almost touching. Most of the early wells were shallow, allowing almost anyone with a little money to drill. Some were drilled by individuals using the ancient spring pole method, a method employing people kicking down the drill bit, letting the pole spring back up, then kicking it down again. But advances were quickly being made in the technology of drilling and casing wells. (API 82, 94-100)

During these first years of the oil boom, Ida Tarbell grew up in the Western Pennsylvania oilfield. Her father, formerly a school teacher and cabinet maker, moved his family to Cherry Run and set up a shop and began making wooden oil tanks. In her autobiography, *All In the Day's Work*, Tarbell tells about life in the oilfield beginning in October of 1860. She was there when the first fountain well came in on April 17, 1861. It was gushing over the derrick when the oil and gas exploded killing the owner of the well, Henry Rouse. She saw her family take in a man, "burned and swollen beyond recognition, yet alive, alive enough to give his name." (ADW 4-8) There were no hospitals, so for weeks her mother nursed the friend, (ADW 8)

Soon other gushers spewed out even more oil. In May, the fountain well on the McElhenny Farm on Oil Creek gushed above its derrick, and there in September, the Empire Well flowed 2,500 barrels a day. The drop in gas pressure in the field soon drove wells on pumps out of business, and the excess production sent prices spiraling downward. In fact, fluctuations in price continued throughout the years of Petrolia production. Whenever prices rose or became stable, new fields were discovered, and prices would plummet.

The gushing or "fountain wells," as they were first called, led to great speculation in oil stocks with people from all over the country rushing to get in on the opportunity to become instantly rich without having to work, the first instances of what came to be called "Oil Fever." It was a ripe field for swindlers who flocked in, sometimes selling more than 100% of a well or selling stock in wells with no chance of being productive.

At first, fear that there was only limited amounts of oil had kept many wary business men from investing in the support of the oil business. From the first, efforts to support and transport oil could not keep up with the discovery and refining of it. Teamsters hauled the first oil from the valley on wagons in leaky barrels. Roads were terrible, often muddy and almost impassable, and freight costs were high, sometimes even exceeding the value of the oil being shipped. Some oil was transported by means of a technique previously used to move timber—a freshet. This was a controlled flood. Lumber companies would cut their dams and the barges with barrels of oil would go rushing downstream on the high water. Sometimes there were disastrous results of this hazardous activity. On May 31, 1864, barge after barge crashed into bridge abutments. Often two thirds of the oil was lost before reaching Pittsburgh. During the six months when the creek was navigable, steamboats were able to move some of the oil.

Over a period of several years, the technology and financing for pipelines gradually improved until it became the main means of getting the oil to the railhead where it could be moved to market. For years, pipelines had moved water and gas, but new techniques had to be discovered to make the oil pipelines work. J. L. Hutchings, inventor of a rotary pump, laid the first pipeline in Pennsylvania in the fall of 1862 — from Tarr farm to a refinery one thousand feet away. This effort was successful, but a larger line, laid further, leaked because of poor cast-iron pipe and bad joints. It was 1864 before the next successful pipeline was laid, one moving refined petroleum three miles from a refinery to the Allegheny River. (API 183-9)

In 1864 there was a major discovery at Pithole, on the upland, leading to major difficulties in moving the crude oil. Samuel Van Syckle began work on forming a company to build a pipeline from Pithole to the railroad five miles away. He succeeded by using fifteen foot joints of wrought iron pipe and welding the joints. In spite of sabotage by teamsters fearing loss of work, Van Syckle completed the project by October of 1865. Soon throughout the region lines were connecting wells to dump tanks and dump tanks to refineries and rail heads.ᵗ

Cover image of *The Devil's Hat*.

Chapter 4

Booming and Blasting

Twenty years passed before the second oil novel was published, *The Devil's Hat: A Sketch in Oil* (1887) by Melville Philips*. It, like most of the early oil novels, was set in the booming oilfields of Western Pennsylvania. *The Devil's Hat* is set in the town of Sandhole, obviously a fictionalized version of the boomtown, Pithole. Pithole began with a gusher on January 7, 1865, grew to a population of 15,000 by September, with banks, churches, a waterworks, a theatre, and fifty hotels. Production fell off sharply and by January, 1866, it was deserted. (*The Early Days of Oil* 6,60)

In Melville Philips' *The Devil's Hat*, a young lawyer, John Ogden, arrives in Sandhole to try to make his fortune. Philips says in his preface that he has first-hand experience in the Pennsylvania oilfield, and he allows Ogden to provide the first detailed account in fiction of the scene there.

> A prospector, "wildcatting" in the depths of the woods, "strikes oil," and in a few days a wondrous life and light burst out in the black silence of the forest. The sun shines on clearings where before a chance ray has not penetrated for half a century. Countless derricks and round red oil-tanks spring up like monster fungi; and presently, ushered by

---

* Philips is the author of several other books including *Snap, a Novel* (1881) and his autobiography, *Recollections* (1891)

the clinking of drills and wheezing of engines, arrive the regular and essential constituents of an oil-town population.

Come the speculators, scouts, landlords, and venders of backwoods necessaries. Then, for a time, the life of the place proceeds swiftly and at high pressure. Saloons, theatres, and churches appear and flourish harmoniously together; but alas! the *delenda est* hurled at Carthage is applicable to every oil-town. The supply of petroleum ebbs, and proportionately to the number of wells sunk in the oil-yielding sand. Then, as the production diminishes, and many fortunes are lost and few won, the unstable community slowly takes flight; the larger hotels close; the theatres and churches are demolished for their lumber; the taverns are removed to freshly discovered fields; a few bankrupt and broken-hearted speculators linger for a while at their "dusters"; but soon the large-eyed owls hoot in entire solitude from the top of the gaunt derricks, while the wind whistles a requiem through the blackened branches of the trees.

The petroleum excitement was at its height; the rage for money-making had taken possession of the soberest minds; husbands encouraged their wives to buy "on margin" with their pin-money; more than one clergyman had dropped his profession to go on 'change at Oil City or Titusville; railroad conductors chatted glibly and incessantly of "flyers" and "certificates"; — and where, then, more likely than to Sandhole, whence issued the most wonderful stories of riches gotten in a day, should an orphan youth of lively imagination drift to seek his fortune? Not since my arrival had I felt so strongly the contagion of the oil-fever as I did on this quiet summer evening. (DH 13-6)

John Ogden meets there a former "fellow student-at-law," Joyce Selden, a man of whom he had formerly had low regard, having considered him "too sober and studious." He now considers him transformed with an engaging manner. He is persuaded by Selden to join with him in drilling a wildcat well. It is to be a "mystery" well. They will be attempting to drill the well without letting others know. They will be drilling on a ridge called The Devil's Hat and will pretend to be building a hotel while hiding a derrick in a depression in the woods. Why the stratagem is necessary is not clear since they have no money to buy other land even if they hit a gusher. Soon after they begin drilling, Ogden is invited to a ball which is to benefit the families of deceased torpedoers.

In 1864 Colonel E. A. L. Roberts had developed a procedure using torpedoes for setting off an explosion at the bottom of a well to fracture the formation and thus get increased production. Colonel Roberts with his brother acquired a patent for the torpedoes, which at first were filled with gunpowder, then nitroglycerin. Many well owners hired "moonshiners," unlicensed, independent operators, since they considered the Roberts' fees exorbitant. (EDO 72-3) Both the transportation and firing of the nitroglycerin was dangerous, particularly for those "moonshiners."

In *The Devil's Hat*, moonshiners are listed prominently among the many inhabitants of the boomtown:

> Then, in the town itself, at the "Bullwheel" hotel—where, when the light and life first burst into the region, and the black solitude of the forest gave way to the blows of the axe, the rattle of machinery, and the roar of the torpedo, you might gladly have paid the price of a suit of clothes for the privilege of catching cold and no sleep, on a mouldy mattress in the cellar—there you will see your fellow-man, in such multiform guises and degrees of mania as you had never dreamed of his assuming. See the broker and "wildcatter," gorgeous of raiment, and mostly profane; the crafty scout, young, intelligent, jolly, but reserved of mien; the calm and wary contractor; the driller, in blue overalls, and blackened of hands and face; the dare-devil torpedoer, blue-shirted, his trousers booted, his hat awry, and his breath redolent of fire-water,—all of these harmoniously commingled. (DH 37)

At the ball Ogden meets one of the few surviving torpedoers, Tickly-Bender, the owner of a wagon that carries the torpedoes, called the "Terror." In the conversation that follows, the wives of some of the deceased torpedoers try to get Tickly-Bender to quit the dangerous occupation: "You're right, Mr. Burns; jus' talk to him. Make him stop 'shinin', and be a reg'lar, if nothing else. The way he fools with glycerine is a sin and a shame. If I was his wife—." (DH 56) But Tickly-Bender, the torpedoer, interrupts them and tells two macabre stories.

> "You folks er unnatcherl timid. I tell you, ye can eat it."
> "Like the girl at '46,'" said Schlau.

"O, yes!" Mrs. Williams assented, "like the girl at '46.'"

"She ran up on the derrick floor," explained Schlau, turning to me, but gazing at TicklyBender, "and dipped her finger in the nitroglycerine, which was almost ready to lower into the well. Then she tripped back to her husband just been married a week—and stuck her finger in her mouth, 'only to taste it'; brought her teeth together, and whoop! off goes her jaw."

"Which I say," commented Tickly, pausing with his knife half-buried in the ham," supposin' it's true, was a dast good thing for her husband."

"You see," said Mrs. Williams, dismally, "what moonshinin' 's brought him to. He's a regular infidel."

"Now, I tell you what it is," Tickly resumed, "glycerine's been a friend to many a man outside o' wildcatters. I knowed one—that's Seth Suttle—over be Warren, that it paid a debt of five hundred dollars for once, by destroyin' the due-bill an' the creditor—that was Parks. They was out walkin' together, an' Parks seen a empty glycerine-can in the road, so he run ahead an' kicked it, 'an' the bucket—as Seth says—together." (DH 57)

A few days later, the driller of Selden and Ogden's well tells them to be prepared to get tanks to catch the oil since they are about to reach the depth where the oil should be if there is any. Ogden goes to Oil City to the exchange to arrange this with Bedford, their contact there. Because they are still trying to keep their well secret, Ogden pretends he is considering a new venture into oil futures in order to cover up his reason for being there. His new friends try to discourage him by telling stories of men who lost everything, men likeone of their group, Sandy:

> "Here's a man, Ogden, who once had a little paradise of a hundred thousand dollars; he lost it; then regained it; then lost it again. On the 11th of December he actually got it back *doubled*; he left 'Change with more than two hundred thousand dollars to his credit, the luckiest dog in town. Then he gave an oyster supper; everybody was there. Sandy opened nearly every bottle of champagne to be had in Oil City; and, after a bit, Mr. Davis says, — 'Sandy, you wouldn't want to buy in any more at $1.08, would you?' — 'Lots of it,' says Sandy — . . . .
>
> '200,000?' says Davis; '500,000!' says Sandy. And he took all that was offered him. The next morning he woke up and heard about the 'gusher' at Balltown, and when he got to 'Change found oil selling at 89, and he owed the market fifty thousand dollars." (DH 69)

Ogden asks Sandy if the story is true. Sandy admits that it is but says that it didn't worry him because he hadn't had time to get his hand on the money any way. Bedford then says that Sandy is a fair example of the whole group and says, "Take my advice: let oil alone; it will burn your fingers." Another of the group, Major Dibbs, disagrees asserting his belief in petroleum: "It is the wonder of the age. I am willing to live and die by it, Bedford. Moreover, I am even anxious to produce it, and give light to the world, as you may have heard." Bedford insists that he will fail: "You and Burns? Yes; but you'll fail, Major! mark my word! Sandhole is a town born of the 'gusher'; has but a few short days to live," (DH 69)

Ogden leaves them and has a harrowing experience on his walk homeward. He is passed by Schlau Burns in a wagon. Burns warns him that Tickly Bender is just behind him and racing him while carrying fifty quarts of nitroglycerin. Ogden sees Tickly-Bender coming but has no time to avoid him. He sees that Tickly is drunk. Then the torpedoer's horse and wagon is upon him:

> The withdrawal of his attention, however brief, from the excited animal — doubtless a slight slack in the tension of the lines — had caused her to swerve towards me, and I fell bodily back as she reared aloft with flashing eyes and distended nostrils — another version of death on the pale horse. I saw the wheels revolving dizzily on the edge of the narrow road, — an inch or two more and they must surely dash against that chestnut stump, — and I shudderingly closed my eyes, with a fluttering fear at my heart of the horrible roar and reverberation that would follow; and, in the second which elapsed, I had a sickening vision of a great opening in the earth and a vast cloud of dust. — A loud oath and laugh from the lips of Tickly-Bender opened my eyes. The team was speeding safely on in the mad race, and as it swung round the curve, out of view, I read, in rude letters, of a brimstone hue, the apt inscription on the rear end of the black box — "The Terror.'" (DH 69)

Finally, Ogden finds something to get excited about. He meets Miss Petrice, a girl who has come to the oil district with her mother who is drilling a well with the help of Major Dibbs. Ogden soon is madly in love with

Petrice. Much of the remainder of the book is about his romance with her, some of which is related to the oilfield. He doesn't seem to have a job at the well, other than messenger boy. He leaves everything to Selden but begins to mistrust him. During a thunderstorm, a bolt of lightning strikes a tank of oil on a ridge above Sandhole. It explodes, kills five people, and catches other tanks on fire. The whole town of Sandhole is imperiled by the wall of burning oil which seems to be certain to move down upon it. Schau Burns comes to the well of Selden and Ogden asking for gunpowder to be used to fire cannons into the tanks in order to empty them and thus keep them from exploding. Ogden agrees to provide the powder but is shocked by his partner's response. Selden says that he has kept back some of the powder. About this Ogden thinks, "Oh, how sorry I was to hear him say this — to see him standing there before me with excited looks, and know the ignoble cause of his anxiety — all oblivious of the lives that were in danger — forgetful of everything save his own imperilled dollars and cents!" (DH 132)

Ogden goes to the well fire with Burns, but as in nearly everything he is an observer standing back watching Burns' attempt to prevent the destruction of the town. He comes to action only when another tank explodes nearby, threatening him and his beloved. He then grabs her and pulls her from danger. She faints as she is prone to do under stress. After the explosion, Selden and Ogden become further estranged. After refusing to sell and take a profit, Selden admits to Ogden that he deceived him at the beginning of their partnership:

"How in the world could you ever suppose that, if I were absolutely certain there was oil here, or if I had possessed the money to develop it,—for I tell you plainly I had only five hundred dollars,—I would come to you and deliberately part with half my interest? I honestly think, Ogden, you are old enough to know that in the world of business no man does another a good turn without valuable consideration—if he is wise. So in this matter of ours. I hadn't the money to execute an idea that took possession of me. You had—otherwise I would certainly have left you out in the cold." (DH 162)

So Ogden plans to get out of the partnership at the first opportunity—even being willing to sign over his portion of the partnership to Selden. A reader might wonder how he is going to provide for himself since he is not eager to practice law. He is not encouraged by Petrice to go after money either. She says that Burns and the Major are too involved with business to be gallant and that they and her mother have the contagion, seeking only "mammon, mammon, mammon." (DH 176) She asks Ogden if he is "oil oily," if he came there to "wildcat or die," if petroleum is his "highest aspiration?"(DH 180) He responds that he is not in love with oil or any speculative business. He fears that he is a "trifler."

It is just as well that he has few ambitions for his oil well because its flow drops to almost nothing. Selden tries to recoup his fortune by playing the oil market and loses even more. Selden engages Tickly-Bender to blast the well in hopes of bringing it back. On the way to town, Ogden meets Tickly-Bender and is offered a ride. He is hesitant until Tickly says the wagon is empty of explosives. As they drive along, he asks Tickly-Bender if he is the oldest torpedoer. Tickly answers, "They ain't no such thing as a old "torpedoer,'" he said, dogmatically. "I never knowed or hear tell of a man gettin' wenerable in the business. But I guess I've lived as long as any 'shiner 'n these parts. The boys say I'm a 'livin' caution'; they say it's unnatschrel, that I ain't got the right to stick out so long." (DH 262-3) He then says that Dick Suttle had tried to bet him that he wouldn't survive a month but that he wouldn't take the bet. Ogden asks him why he doesn't drop the business and take up a healthier one, but he grins and says, "The trouble is, I'm a-thinkin', that all of us fellows believes every one else but hisself's a-goin' to bust. Now, I used to think it was purty ticklish work to smuggle glycerine up here from town. We brung it on the trains, in grip-sacks. But Lor'! now, that 'd be nothin'." (DH 262-3) He says that thirteen men started moonshining together and after a year only three of them survived: "You see, I got so I didn't mind the goin' to pieces, what the papers call the 'sickenin' details' — it was the lonesomeness." (DH 263) At first, his wife worried, but she has become used to it. She wouldn't let him carry his watch so that when he was blown up, he wouldn't be wasting what little property he had.

Then Tickly-Bender tells his two friends what happened:

> "Then, they was three of us left—Bill Tuppin, Tom Picks, an' me. We used to talk about it together, an' Bill 'd say, 'Tickly, you're the next one, sure

as shootin', if you ain't more partickler lowerin' the cans'; an' I'd say, 'Tom Picks, if you don't drive yer mare with a tighter rein, you're agoin' up, sure'; an' I guess Tom pitied both me an' Bill, for he never said much. But purty soon Bill swore he b'lieved thirteen had been a unlucky number, an' said he was goin' to get a place with the 'reg'lars.' An' he did. That was at Tidioute; an' one day Tom an' me was talkin' to the superintender of the torpedo company, when Bill druv by with fifty quarts aboard, goin' towards the magazine, a iron safe that stood over 'n a clearin.' The superintender was blowin' to me an' Tom 'bout what a bulge his company had on the railroads in accidents to the men. 'There's no damages lowed the family,' says he, 'an' as there's hardly any remains, we ain't even got the funeral expenses to pay.' After a bit, there was the usule noise over be the woods. The superintender jumped three feet, an' swore. 'Fifty quarts, by George! ' says he. We walked over, an', as as we was going', Tom turns to him an' says, 'If Bill's gone up, gimme his job?' 'Mebbe,' says the boss; 'but, I tell ye, you'll have to be more partickler 'n Bill. He's the fifth man this month, makin' a total loss of more 'n five hundred quarts. The company can't stand sech nonsense.'

"Sure enough, there was a nasty hole 'n the ground, but not a sign of Bill or his team. Purty soon we saw some bits of the wagon up in the trees, an' the superintender found a bit of meat, dry and scorched. Them was all. 'Is it man or horse?' says Tom; and dast if we could tell. No more could Bill's wife, but she run the risk, an' buried it."

"Horrible! " I said.

Tickly-Bender was pleased with my exclamation.

"Why," he continued, in a boasting tone, "I once helped to pick up what was left of five busted torpedoers. They on'y half filled a cigarbox. You should uv seen the five widders family, sortin' the pieces! Why, they cried an' jangled over the most decent-lookin' chunks of meat, till Mrs. Punkey got the prize package. It was a part of a rib, an' she was tremenjous proud about it; for, she says, 'it's not horse, any way.'" (DH 264-6)

Ogden asks if Tom Picks is still alive, and Tickly-Bender tells him that he is not, "not by a jugful," leaving Tickly the only surviving moonshiner of the thirteen. Without a smile, he tells Ogden, "We buried him in a tomat' can, but as we wasn't certain if we had him or his horse, the boys wrote on the lid with a nail: — 'Tom Picks, or Driller, his mare.'" (DH 266)

As Ogden leaves, he advises Tickly to give up his profession if he is to live, telling him that he is sitting on the lid of a volcano. In response to this Tickly breaks into laughter and says: "So was you. There's easily a hundred quarts in the box now. I told you there wasn't any, 'cause I wanted you to feel comfortable." (DH 267) With this final word, Tickly goes laughing, spinning off in the "Terror."

Soon after, Tim, the driller, tells Ogden that the well is dry and that that night they will use a torpedo on it. Ogden discovers that most people are moving out of Sandhole for Fordell, the newest boom area. He also finds that the mother of his beloved has sold her well to Major Dibbs and that they have left Pennsylvania, mainly because of an old scandal of which the mother is innocent. Ogden is heartbroken as he returns to the well to conclude his business with Selden. He starts toward the well when he hears an explosion. The whole crew and Tickly-Bender are blown to bits. Selden, though wounded, survives. Ogden and his friend, Professor Talcott, leave for Europe in hopes of seeing Petrice and her mother. After two years they meet them again, and Ogden finally is happy, particularly since he finds out his former partner has been arrested for embezzlement and is in jail. How Ogden is making a living is never explained.

This novel, the first one set in an oilfield, has the people actively involved in the drilling and torpedoing of wells. There is little information about the drilling, but much about how quickly the boom towns come and go. The major characters are flat and predictable. John is hardly someone Petrice would be interested in. She is much like Phillis Fleming—young, pretty, intelligent, open, upper class, but rather conventionally Victorian. Though the characters are flat, *The Devil's Hat* succeeds at several levels, particularly in its humorous depiction of the dangers of torpedoing.

Chapter 5

More Blasting

Prince Dusty by Kirk Munroe, the third oilfield novel, was published in 1891. It was one of a series of adventure books written by Munroe for children. In it he allows the twelve-year-old hero, Arthur Dale Dustin, to engage in adventure after adventure, some of which relate to the oilfield. Arthur is in the oilfield because his parents have died, and he has come to live with his father's brother, who works as a driller in the Pennsylvania oilfield. Arthur's Aunt mistreats him but allows him lots of freedom.

One of his friends, Brace Barlow, a former employee of his uncle, has been working as a moonshiner like Tickly-Bender of *The Devil's Hat*. Arthur has pleaded with him to give up the work, but Brace has said that he has as much right as anyone else to risk death. Besides it is the easiest way to make good money.

But soon after this discussion Brace has a close call:

> Then Brace told him that about an hour before, he had been driving quietly along, with fifty quarts of nitroglycerine stowed snugly under his buggy seat, toward a well that he was to shoot at daylight, when the sound of galloping hoofs gave warning that a detective was on his track. He instantly whipped up his horses, and, as they sprang forward his light buggy was nearly upset by striking some obstacle,

and he was thrown to the ground with such force as to be partially stunned. As he lay there the detective dashed past without noticing him, and overtaking the runaway team a minute later probably tried to stop them. They must have swerved to one side, the buggy had undoubtedly been upset and a terrific explosion instantly followed. (PD 26-7)

When Brace reached the scene everything was blown up—horse, wagon, and detective. There was only a great hole in the ground.

Soon after this event, Arthur persuades Brace to take him with him to a well shooting. Brace drives more slowly that usual. Arthur helps carry the tin tubes to the well and helps him unwind two-thousand feet of cord to be used to let down the torpedo into the well: ". . . the line was run through a pulley that hung directly above the well, and its end terminating in an iron hook, dangled close to the mouth of the deep dark hole." (PD 27) Then Brace fastens together fifty feet of tin pipe to make the anchor in order to support the torpedo fifty feet above the bottom. Arthur helps Brace make these preparations, but Arthur and all the men working on the well and Arthur have to leave when Brace starts pouring the explosive into the torpedo. The men go farther away than Arthur. Brace begins the more dangerous part of the job:

> At this time the empty shell, which was a large tin tube about twenty feet long, was with its anchor attached, hanging in the well so that its upper end was just above the surface. It hung from a very shallow iron hook, at the end of the stout cord arranged

for the purpose; and Brace Barlow now proceeded slowly and cautiously to pour the nitroglycerine into it. The stuff was the color of soft soap, and about as thick as syrup. (PD 27-8)

After a few minutes, Arthur hears Brace call for help, asking someone to come quickly. Arthur goes to his aid at once. Brace says he hadn't meant him but that he might do. Brace tells him the hook has slipped off the shell and that he has caught the shell to keep it from falling and exploding before he is ready. Brace tells what has happened and what needs to be done:

> Then the weight of the cord pulled the hook up so that I can't reach it. Now if you climb up the side of the derrick holding the drill rope in close to you till you reach the proper height, then swing out, catch hold of the hook, and slide down the drill rope with it in your hand, you will do what I want as well as if you were the biggest man in the world. (PD 31)

Arthur immediately climbs the derrick. The torpedo is so heavy that Brace can't support it very long. Arthur "forgetting all thoughts of danger," (PD 31) quickly climbs the derrick, swings out on the drill rope, secures the hook, and slides down with it. Then instead of giving it to Brace, "he stepped boldly up and attached it to the copper bail of the torpedo that was cutting deep into the flesh of the strong hand that held it, and must in another minute have let it go. (PD 31) Brace drops the go devil on the torpedo. The well explodes and gushes. And Brace tells Arthur that he has saved his life.

Dusty and Phin pole to safety in *Prince Dusty*.

Chapter 5 51

But all does not go well at his Uncle's house. He has bullying cousins who are pretending that they are blowing up a well and put a firecracker under their sister's cat. Arthur runs up and prevents the cruelty, and his older cousin starts to beat him. He is rescued by his parents' former servant and former slave, Uncle Phinn.

Arthur is punished by his aunt. And Uncle Phinn who has been doing odd jobs to pay for his keep is no longer welcomed there. So Phinn and Arthur set out penniless for West Virginia where Arthur's grandfather, Colonel Dale, lives. They have many adventures and hardships on the way, only one of which involves oil. While rafting down the river toward Pittsburgh on the Allegheny, they stop briefly at a pumping station and visit with the friendly engineer and his family. While there, a storm comes up and lightning strikes the oil tanks, and a surge of burning oil comes rushing toward them. Arthur grabs an ax and cuts the rope holding them to the shore. He and Phinn pole their craft mightily and are barely able to escape the flames which come onto the river and burn all about them.

Arthur and Phinn finally arrive at his grandfather's farm. After a cheerful welcome, Arthur learns that his grandfather is having great financial difficulties. Arthur tells his grandfather that he has inherited twenty-five acres from his father and that they should try to drill an oil well on it. The grandfather says that he knows nothing about oil wells. Arthur explains:

> "That's just it, sir! And it is because both of us are "chumps' that we'll be certain to strike oil. Brace

Barlow always says so. You see, a 'chump' is someone who does n't know any more about oil, or where to find it, than we do. What Brace Barlow says is, that while those who know about the business often strike 'dusters' a 'genuine chump,' always has luck his first well." (PD 218)

Grandfather Dale finally agrees to undertake the venture and borrows money on his estate to make the attempt. This will be a true wildcat because it is some distance from another well. Colonel Dale studies up on petroleum, and there are several pages where he is given an opportunity to provide an oil history, even including information about Hugh Nixon Shaw's discovery in Canada.

Cousin Hatty is given the task of siting the well because the Colonel has learned too much and is not sufficiently a chump any more. Hatty picks a spot that she could see from her room. Colonel Dale goes to the oil region to buy equipment and hires Brace Barlow as his driller. As they begin to drill, the reader gets a detailed explication of how an oil well is drilled. (PD 243-4)

Then we learn of the progress of their well:

> Day after day the powerful drills worked steadily downward through hard and soft rock, sometimes descending only six or eight feet in twenty-four hours, but generally cutting through twenty or thirty feet of material in a day. The first and second sandstones or "sands" were passed, and at length the drill was down a thousand feet. At this depth it had not yet reached the third, or oil-bearing sandstone. Occasional puffs of gas came up through the

casing of iron pipe that was driven down as fast as the hole was cut to receive it; but there was no sign of oil. (PD 264)

After two months of drilling, Colonel Dale has spent most of his money and is very worried. Since this is a wildcat, there are numerous scouts around to see whether a gusher will change the price of oil. Colonel Dale is working with a broker in Oil City and will provide him with the earliest information about the success or failure of the well. The well is boarded up to prevent information about it from getting out.

When the appropriate depth is reached and there is no oil, Brace stops drilling, and it appears the well is a duster. Colonel Dale goes to his room and sits alone depressed. Early next morning, Arthur is wakened by Brace. Brace has a load of nitroglycerine and a torpedo. Arthur says that he thought that the torpedoes were only used to explode producing wells to get them to produce more. Brace says that that is true but that he is convinced that there is oil down this hole and the charge may cause it to come up. Arthur gives him permission to blast. Brace says that he is going to use a bigger shot than he has ever used before and that it can't do any harm and might do some good. Already on the scene are two tanks capable of holding a thousand gallons. The casing head is ready as is the oil saver.

Arthur helps Brace in the dangerous work of preparing the torpedo. In an hour they are ready. Arthur gets to drop it:

With the utmost coolness and steadiness of

nerve, 'Prince Dusty' held the iron-winged messenger of destruction over the mouth of the well for an instant, and then sped it on its downward flight, toward the monster waiting a thousand feet below to receive it. (PD 263)

Then came trembling like an earthquake, a roar—then silence. Next a liquid column rose slowly to about twenty feet and fell back. Then came a black column of mud, water, and burned glycerine to the top of the derrick. The black included some yellowness of oil. then a "dense volume of gas burst forth" and then it came:

> As this cleared away there stood revealed a solid golden column, six inches in diameter, reaching to the top of the derrick and breaking into great jets and fountains of amber-colored spray against the crown pulley. (PD 264)

Arthur is sent racing to the telegraph office five miles away with a coded message for Colonel Dale's oil broker. Meanwhile, Brace is trying to bring the well under control, for the oil is being wasted:

> At length, under a pressure of nearly three thousand pounds, the oil-saver was slowly forced down upon the fierce stream until its cap finally met the casing head. A moment later the set screws were turned, and the torrent of oil was discharging into the waiting tanks. Its force was as great as though it were impelled by the pump of a steam fire-engine, and the pipes through which it discharged throbbed and vibrated under the terrible pulsations of the flow. (*PD* 365)

Chapter 5   55

The tanks began to fill rapidly, and supposedly they were able to construct a pipeline quickly to send the overflow into the tanks of the pipeline and on to the distant refineries.

Soon "Prince Dusty" is a true oil prince. He and his family are immensely rich and start being philanthropic.

This is another Victorian novel better at describing the tools and procedures of the oilfield than it is at describing the social relationships of its characters. Most of these relationships are written about melodramatically and floridly. But there are some nicely drawn adventures here.

Gas and water come before the oil in *Prince Dusty*

Chapter 6

Two Short Stories

Also showing torpedoing in a booming oil town in Pennsylvania is W. B. Atkinson's "Charlie Ransom," a long short story in *Western Stories*, a collection of short stories published in Edinburgh in 1893. In the novella length account of fifty-two pages, we have a story of love and tragedy. The oil town of Pan Handle City has been prosperous for six years, and its residents are in need of a school and teacher. They build a school and succeed in hiring a beautiful young teacher, Marie Reese. When winter arrives, some of the older boys and young oil men idled by the weather start taking her class. One of those is Charlie Ransom, sometimes called The Doll because he is so cute. He falls in love with Marie and buys her skates so that they can skate together. She feels only friendship for him and is already engaged to John Burlington of Philadelphia. When Charlie Ransom falls ill with "brain fever," she helps nurse him and even plants a sympathetic kiss on his cheek. He interprets this as a show of love on her part. She sings to him to cheer him up. He begins to get well. Spring comes and with it her fiancé. Charlie is miserable and jealous and hates John Burlington. The oil business comes more directly into the plot when the narrator explains in detail how nitroglycerin is used in torpedoing a well.

A shooter successfully explods a well but inadvertently leaves a small red container of nitroglycerin in a public boat. Not knowing this, Burlington gets into the boat. Ransom sees him:

> Ransom, who was standing perhaps twenty yards away, also saw the red can; but, unlike Burlington, he knew full well that it contained some of the deadly nitro-glycerine — knew that it was a can which the 'shooting-fiend' had, in his hurry to get away, forgotten. He knew, too, that the creek was full of huge masses of ice which the spring thaw had loosened. Ransom was perfectly aware of all the dangers which Burlington hazarded in crossing the swollen creek, and was quite conscious of the awful possibility of a collision, in which case the boat and its occupant must meet with total annihilation. All this Ransom knew, yet uttered never a word of caution. What was it to him? He did not place the can in the boat; the dynamite was not his, nor the boat either, neither was he responsible for John Burlington's safety. (WS 45-6)

Burlington's boat explodes, and he is seriously injured but survives. Almost immediately Charlie feels regret and guilt. He goes to Marie, tells her what he has done, and asks for her forgiveness, but she will not forgive him. He returns to his room desolate. But soon he has a chance to make amends.

Because of the success of the first torpedoing, most of the oil producers have their wells exploded and soon seven or eight wells are gushing:

> All the owners of unsatisfactory wells had them immediately 'shot;' and within two days after the accident to John Burlington, seven or eight wells

were throwing huge fountains of oil which it was impossible for a time to control. This oil, which was nearly all wasted, flowed in every direction about Pan Handle City, finally finding its way to the Tomhicken Creek. Meanwhile, locomotion was difficult, and where practicable, exceedingly disagreeable; for some of the streams of crude oil were as much as ten feet wide and several inches deep. (WS 54)

Marie is left alone in danger from the flowing oil:

The house stood upon a small and slight elevation, which, being directly in the course of an overflow of waste petroleum, divided the stream into two currents, each of them six or seven feet wide. These joined their forces once more just below the house, thus temporarily transforming the hillock into a little island. (WS 55)

Then a fire threatens Marie:

In the dead of the night, from some unaccountable cause — in the oil regions the origin of a fire is never discovered — a fire broke out near the very well from which the stream flowed around Peter Lamson's house, and in less than one minute a mighty river — or wall of fire ten feet wide and ten feet high, was rolling onward toward the Tomhicken. It had come to Pan Handle City at last — one of those fearful fire-scourges, immunity from which is guaranteed to none of the oil towns and villages; and it had come, as they usually do, when the men were least prepared to combat it. (WS 55-6)

Charlie runs through a wall of fire to reach Marie.

He wraps her in his coat and carries her back through the stream of fire. She escapes with minor burns, but he is near death. He asks her forgiveness again. This times she forgives him. Then she sings a song to him, one which begins, "My heavenly home is bright and fair." (WS 59) And he dies.

"Charlie Ransom" is not great literature as this summary and these excerpts reveal, but it is an important early work describing life in the Pennsylvania oilfield.

Just three years after "Charlie Ransom" appeared in Western Stories in Edinburgh, Scotland, "In the Virginias" (1896) a collection of stories by Waitman Barbe* appeared in America. It's a much shorter story, eleven small pages, having little detail about the oil business. It is a rather general moral tale with an O. Henry twist at the end. There are no scenes. Most of the story is presented in summary.

John Richards, an old hermit, holds twenty-five acres near a new oilfield. The primary owner of the land, Fleming McDonald, wants the hermit's land. The conflict is introduced in a couple of paragraphs

> The oil excitement grew in intensity as the wells came nearer to the neighborhood in which John Richards lived; but he paid no attention to it, except to refuse all offers to lease or buy his twenty-acre lot.
>
> One day a derrick was erected on the edge of a lot adjoining his, and pretty soon the "bird of the

---

*Waitman Barbe was a graduate of the University of West Virginia and a long time member of and chair of its English department. He was the author of several collections of poetry.

walking-beam," so familiar to oil operators, began to sing its monotonous song. As the drill went down the excitement went up, for only a short distance away men who, a year before, were not worth a dollar, now had an income of fifty or a hundred dollars a day.

The strata were carefully examined, and a logbook of the well was kept by a geologist—Prof. W.—who had located the well, and who was expecting it to extend the territory. At last the third sand was reached, and the well was "shot." It proved to be a geniune "gusher," making seven hundred barrels in twenty-four hours. (In the Virginias 135-6)

McDonald has come to the oilfield in West Virginia with his three daughters, been fortunate, and become rich. He lives like a king and his daughters have horses and carriage and a luxurious life. He wants to get control of the entire field. He tries many kinds of dirty tricks to convince the old hermit to lease his lands. It is generally believed that he had offered gold to anyone who will kill Richards. Then he tries to get a crooked lawyer to draw up papers claiming that Richards doesn't have clear title to the land. But this too fails.

Finally McDonald gives up trying to get the land. And shortly afterward his luck begins to turn. His wells become depleted and his new attempts mostly dry. He becomes more desperate and reckless and eventually is ruined financially. He never tells his daughters of his trouble, and he goes to the stable and shoots himself. The three girls see all their wealth vanish.

Soon afterwards John Richards leases his land:

His thoughts were entirely taken up with his well. He took more interest in it than he had shown in anything before for forty years. Every day the old man, with his long white hair, could be seen watching the progress of the bit as it bored its way into the earth. He even became communicative, and, as there began to appear favorable signs of the right kind and quantity of sand, his face would light up and he would hobble around and talk about his good luck.

When the oil sand was pierced, and the oil spouted over the derrick, he fairly danced for joy, and his old wrinkled face seemed to lose its wrinkles and to beam with delight. It proved to be the best well in the county, and before sundown the old man was offered once more a big sum of money for his little patch of ground. But he replied; "Come around in the morning." (IV 143)

When the people came around the next day his cabin is empty and on a table is a note that reads: " I am going away and will not return. Look under the last plank in the floor."(IV 143) And they found there the last will of John Richards "written with his own hand an hour after he had struck the well." The last sentence of the story is "The old man had bequeathed his twenty-acre lot to the penniless daughters of his old enemy and persecutor." (IV 144)

Now that is a weird ending. If Richards is still alive what good is a will to the girls? I guess Waitman Barbe didn't worry about the little technicalities, nor did he worry about motivation. Nothing in the story even suggested that Richards was aware that his oppressor even had daughters.

Of the two stories "Charley Ransom" is decidedly better in spite of its sentimentality.

Cover image of *The Wild-Catters*.

Chapter 7

A Young Englishman In the Oilfield

Like *The Devil's Hat*, the fourth oil novel, *The Wild-Catters: A Tale of the Pennsylvanian Oil Field* by C. J. Cutliffe Hyne* published in England in 1895 is most emphatic about the boom-and-bust nature of oil towns. The protagonist, a young Englishman, George Hathaway, arrives in Cherry Grove, Pennsylvania in May 1882, as the town is coming to be. Just days earlier, the first wildcat had been drilled there. George has come to make his fortune. He meets Hiram J. Staines almost immediately, and Staines offers him a job. George says he needs to look around first. Staines says, "Hurry, or the town may be gone again before you've seen half of it. We oilmen ain't got time to consider over things. We have to act when the idea's hot in us."(W-C 13) While checking the countryside, George prevents a young man, Dick Oswald, from being beaten and makes a friend of him. When Dick finds out that George is considering investing his small capital in an oil well, Dick tells George to get advice from Staines. But George, acting on his own, buys a well from an honest-looking man, Mr. Frettleby. George soon discovers that he has been deceived and that Frettleby is

---

* Hyne, 1865 – 1944, is the author of over sixty novels and is best known for his science-fiction novel, *The Lost Continent*.

a well-known con man. George tries to make the well pay by torpedoing it and thus spends most of his remaining capital without getting any more oil.

George and Dick go to work as scouts for Staines to find out whether Frettleby has struck oil at his wildcat well. They are almost killed in the attempt but finally discover that it is a good well. But by the time they get the information to Staines, everyone has the same information, so it is of no use to Staines.

George scouts for Staines in *The Wild-Catters*

George takes his last one hundred dollars and joins Dick Oswald in the mercantile business. They make a go of it for a while, but the store catches fire, and they escape with only three crowbars, a few cans of meat, and their skins. They sell the crowbars and decide to take some time off and just wander around and camp. While wandering deep in the wilderness, they come upon a creek that has oil floating on top. They are convinced that it is a good place to drill a well, but having no money, they go looking for a capitalist to back them. After meeting with no success, they remember their former employer, Staines. Unfortunately Staines, known for making and losing many fortunes, has just had two disasters. Two of his oil storage tanks have exploded, and his mansion has been washed away in a flood. The young men approach him anyway and discover that he still has enough capital to back them, but just barely. They will have to do all the work themselves. Staines has an agent buy the land for them and secure leases on neighboring property.

Hyne provides a detailed account of how one constructs a drilling rig in a wilderness. George and Staines set up a circular saw and build a shanty and a derrick. Then they enclose everything because they will be drilling during the winter. Dick makes several trips freighting the boiler and drill equipment to the place. Then we get the first detailed account of drilling equipment in a work of fiction, a cable-tool rig:

> A drive-pipe had been forced down through the earth to the rock, and on the day when Dick returned from Clarendon, after taking back his empty waggon for the last time, the boring was regularly begun. To the end of the rope over the pulley at the head of the derrick was made fast the "ropesocket," then the "sinker-bar," next the "jars" (two heavy bars linked together), then the eight-foot long "auger-stem," and finally the "bit" itself, a long bar of steel as heavy as a man could lift, star-pointed at the end, where it had to cut and pound the rock.

This long string of iron was lowered down into the hole already made in the earth, and the huge rude "walking-beam" of the engine began to pump them monotonously up and down.

As the rock beneath was bitten away, the "temperscrew" lowered the apparatus down inch by inch, and at every six feet of drive the hole was hoisted out by a big windlass called the "bull-wheel"; and then a small winch, yclept the "sand-reel," lowered down the sand-pump, a cylinder with valves, which removed the detritus, and the "bailer," which took up the water, if there chanced to be any.

Once started, the work took but little attention. The engine was governed by a simple arrangement of strings from inside the derrick-house; and the hand who did this could also attend to the temper-screw, and go outside occasionally to do the necessary stoking to the boiler. Indeed, in most wells a "oneman shift " is considered ample to look after the actual boring, so the twenty-four hours were divided into four-hour watches, and as there were three individuals to take these up, each had a change every day. (W-C 192-5)

The three devise a procedure for damming a ravine in order to store the oil when it comes. They work regularly, drilling deeper and deeper, and have no difficulty reaching the depth for setting casing:

"Three hundred feet," announced Staines one day, after totting up the number of turns the bull-wheel had made in hauling the boring irons out of the well. "Three hundred feet, and a good deal of water getting into the well from veins in the rock. I guess we'll just use sand-pump and bailer, and get her nicely cleaned out, and then put the casing in without further delay. It won't do to get swamped. Water's a very good thing in its way, but it's a nuisance when it meddles with an oil-well."

So the "casing," a six-inch iron tube, was joined together length by length, and lowered gradually into the bore-hole, and then the "bit," the auger-stem," the "jars," and all their ponderous accompaniment were again sent down to do their work under the persuasion of that never-tiring walking-beam. (W-C 199-200)

Somehow our heroes know how to do all the jobs though none had any experience in drilling a well. Nor do they have any accidents. Their main difficulty is that they are on short rations, having spent all their available money. As they pass the depth where oil should have been according to their calculations, they grow increasingly despondent. Staines and George consider giving up and calling it a duster, but Dick persists. As the others begin to pack to leave, the well begins to gush. While they are trying to bring it under control, they look up and see their old nemesis, Mr. Frettleby. He drives hastily away. They finally manage to turn the oil into their ravine-tank. Worn out from their efforts, they sleep for thirteen hours. When they get up again, they are surprised to find that their tank is about to overflow. They quickly start another tank below the first by using axes and shovels. They cut down trees then cover them with dirt. They even pull down a whole embankment to support their makeshift dam.

After meeting this crisis, they discover that Fret-

Chapter 7   69

tleby has returned with two armed henchmen. He threatens to kill them if they don't sign over the well and their land to him. They manage to get inside the derrick without being shot. There they brace themselves in and, armed with iron bars, prepare to fight. The gang starts pulling the boards off the side of the derrick house. The two hired hands refuse to go through the hole they have made:

> But Frettleby settled it. To give the man his due, he was plucky to the end of his fat fingers, and so, rushing at the breach, he pressed his big body through. But the point of entrance was where the engine lay, and in coming through, the man had laid hold of one of the cords which governed its movements. That cord, as it happened, led to a throttle-valve; and, before any one clearly saw what was happening, steam had been turned on, the ponderous walking-beam had descended with remorseless force, and all that remained of the intruder was a crushed and mutilated corpse. (W-C 227-8)

That is a fitting end for a villain in an oil novel. Our heroes pick up his pistol, and the other two gang members run away, all the while threatening to return and get their revenge. But before they can do so, the word of the discovery has somehow gotten out, and our three heroes are swamped immediately with people arriving with money wanting to buy everything. Upon Staines advice, they agree to wait and hold an auction where they will sell it all. Even before they sell, people are coming in and starting to build a town. The state surveyor explains:

"This yer township's been christened Oswaldville, after the original locator," he said, "if you other two pardners are agreeable; and now I'll thank you to give me any ideas you may have about laying it out. I guess you'll have to jump lively, though, if I'm to use your notions up, as the whole plan's got to be done under the hour. The chaps can't be expected to wait longer than that. They'd begin to run the town up straight away if there wasn't a picture ready by then. Now I suppose you'd like this original clearing for the site of the Town Hall and People's Palace, with Main Street running east and west slick through it. That's the usual thing." The surveyor worked with pen and ruler, and got his suggestions on paper as he went along. "And then we'll have some half dozen roads across lots either way. That'll be enough to begin upon. You can step around and name them after your friends when they're marked out. And then we might have the railroad depot here. No? There? Oh, very well; that'll do. And the Pipe Line office alongside? Yes. And public buildings? oh yes, we'll pepper them up and down Main Street. Look! — Post Office, Telephone Exchange, Mechanics' Institute, Church — we might have a road running out to the cemetery alongside that; and then here comes your Town Hall, on the other side of which we'll have Bank, Oil Exchange, Cable Agency, a couple of hotels opposite one another to keep their prices down, and the rest we'll leave to fill in as they're wanted. Now I call that a nice modest beginning. It brings bad luck on a place to plot it out on too large a scale at first. So long. Guess I won't detain you gentlemen any longer." And off the surveyor went to measure and peg out the town which he had so glibly specificated." (W-C 13)

The three partners have their auction and sell their holdings for a million each — three millionaires. They have to move out of their shanty, so they seek a room in the new Grand Hotel of All Nations. The clerk explained a difficulty:

> "Private sitting-room, gentlemen? No, we haven't got one at liberty at present; in fact, we haven't one in the hotel; but if you'll just step into the bar, I'll send word to the carpenter, and build you a beauty in two hours."
>
> They laughed and went. The room took a trifle longer than that to build, and the furniture was crude when it was finished, and the pervading smell obtrusively new; . . . . (W-C 248)

The three millionaires leave town on the newly built railroad. Staines offers to continue in business with the two young men, but they choose to return to England to live off the income from their new wealth. Staines agrees to visit them there for a trip to Europe.

This is the only oil novel I know which has no love interest. Indeed, there are no women in the novel, no mention of one except for George's mother to whom he is returning. But it sets the standard for many oil novels to follow in that it gives details of drilling although their drilling is not fraught with the many difficulties, accidents, and dangers of the typical oil novel.

Chapter 8

Rockefeller and the Standard

Several early oil novels concern Standard Oil and its practices in the oilfields. In several also, there is a villainous character modeled on John D. Rockefeller. Before considering these novels, it is helpful to see how Standard and Rockefeller operated in the early days of American oil.

John D. Rockefeller understood the importance of controlling the transportation and refining of oil. Initially his companies invested nothing in producing oil but worked with the railroads to control the distribution. Rockefeller was in a commodities business with Maurice Clark in Cleveland in 1863 when Samuel Andrews approached the partners about setting up a refinery. Andrews had been refining lard oil and coal oil for C. A. Dean in Cleveland and began refining petroleum for him in 1860. Andrews was taken into the Clark and Rockefeller company, and the company built its first refinery on Kingsbury Run, a small stream which emptied into the Cuyahoga River, and thus enabled them to ship by water through the Erie Canal. Later that year, trains of the Atlantic and Great Western Railroad reached Cleveland, providing the new refinery with access to the oilfields of Pennsylvania and railroad connections to New York, and ultimately the opportunity to ship kerosene to the world markets. (*Titan* 79-80)

Rockefeller's recent biographer, Ron Chernow,

sees Rockefeller's success as growing from his "overmastering need for order" (T80) set off against the chaos of the early oil business. Rockefeller later talked about the helter skelter way business was conducted. He hated the extreme fluctuations in price of oil brought on by gluts, with prices, for example, skidding from $3 a barrel to 10¢. Rockefeller, a sober, strict Baptist, visited the oilfield once, in 1863, and was apparently appalled by what he saw of boomtown life, the rampant immorality of brothel and tavern. (T84)

In 1865, Rockefeller bought out two of his partners, Maurice and James Clark, and joined with Samuel Andrews in setting up a new firm. They soon built another refinery, The Standard Works. Rockefeller was successful for several reasons. He manufactured his own barrels, using kiln-dried lumber, reducing weight and shrinkage and thus waste. He also sold by-products: benzine, paraffin, and petroleum jelly. (T100)

By 1866, two thirds of the kerosene from Cleveland's many refineries was being shipped overseas. The buyers from France and Germany were essentially controlling the price of kerosene. Whenever they heard of a glut in oil production, they stopped buying until the price came down. To counter this, Rockefeller sent his brother William, to New York to set up a branch office and to keep abreast of kerosene prices so that the company could buy more or less oil. William was also in charge of getting money from New York bankers to finance their expansion. As a result of some of John D. Rockefeller's borrowing, he took on a new partner in 1867, Henry Flagler. Flagler and Rockefeller worked amicably for years in spite of Flagler's at times headstrong determination. It was Flagler who negotiated the controversial deals the company made with railroads. (T 109)

Freight cost was pivotal in the success or failure of a refinery. In warm weather, Rockefeller could ship oil by water to New York cheaper than he could by rail, so the railroads, to get his business, would reduce their rates. Therefore, he could use the circuitous route of bringing the oil from Western Pennsylvania to Cleveland and then to New York City and still ship his products more cheaply than those producers shipping by a more direct route. Several rail lines serviced Cleveland: New York Central, Erie, and The Pennsylvania. Flagler and Rockefeller were masters at playing one line against the others in order to get special treatment. By 1868, they had received concessions from all the major railroads, some providing rebates of as much as 75%. In one of these deals, Rockefeller agreed to ship by a New York Central subsidiary 60 carloads of refined oil daily. Because Rockefeller was already Cleveland's largest refiner, he was able to make these guarantees and thus get the large rebates, allowing him to make more money and thus make his company grow larger. Rebates by railroads had been a common practice for years, but no other refiners received rebates as high and for as long as Rockefeller and Flagler. (T 107-17)

A five-year depression hit the oil business in the late 1860s, and Rockefeller seized the opportunity to replace competition with cooperation. In 1870, refining capacity was triple the amount of crude oil being produced. He decided to buy up refineries in order to curtail the overproduction. To do this, he needed capital, so Flagler suggested that they incorporate. Thus, Standard Oil Company (Ohio) was born. At the time, Standard "controlled 10 percent of all American Petroleum Refining as well as a barrel-making plant, warehouses, shipping facilities, and a fleet of tank cars." (T132)

Standard began its march toward dominance by buying up companies and retaining the original names while having the companies deny any connection to Standard. One of the first purchased in this fashion was J. A. Bostwick and Company, the premier oil buyer in New York. Then, in January 1872, Standard raised its capital from one million to 3.5 million by taking in new large shareholders. With this new money, Standard began to buy up the other Cleveland refineries.

At this time, too, Rockefeller signed on to a plan put forth by Tom Scott of the Pennsylvania railroad, by which he and a few other refiners would get incredibly favorable benefits from the railroads. The railroads would raise their rates, would give these favored refiners a 40 percent rebate, would pay these refiners 40 cents for each barrel of oil shipped by their competitors, and would inform them of when and how much oil was shipped by the competitors. Many of the major oil companies signed on to the agreement to be managed by the South Improvement Company (SIC), a company controlled by Rockefeller and his fellow Standard shareholders. The agreement would kill the refineries in Titusville and Oil City, and those affected in the oil region took to the street to fight it, led by

John Archbold. The oil producers embargoed the sale of crude oil to those in the South Improvement Company. The controversy ended when Scott and the other railroad leaders, after meeting with excluded refiners, agreed to end the unfavorable pricing.

Though the SIC never functioned, it was used as a threat by Standard to enable it to buy twenty-two of the twenty-six Cleveland refineries between February 17 and March 28, leaving them with control of all their major competitors there. Following the demise of the SIC, Rockefeller developed another cartel with the Pittsburgh refiners in order to control production and prices, but cheaters often exceeded their quota. In June 1873, Rockefeller dissolved the cartel. Meanwhile, producers had formed their own cartel to try to control production. But even with threats of nighttime raids, the producers were not able to control the production of their members, and non members took advantage of the opportunity to undersell the members.

When a six-year depression began in 1873, Rockefeller seized the opportunity to move from city to city absorbing competitors and having them continue to operate under their own name—from Pittsburgh to Philadelphia and on to New York. By hiring his former competitors, he kept them from starting new refineries to compete with him. Rockefeller sometimes used pressure to force his competitors to sell—for example by buying all the barrels in an area or by monopolizing all the available tank cars. In 1874, Rockefeller moved into the oil region itself, buying the Imperial Refining Company in Oil City, and then in 1875, he bought the second largest refiner and with it came John Archbold, future President of Standard. In 1875, Standard formed the Acme Oil Company as a front to buy oil region refineries, and within the year, Archbold bought twenty-seven refineries. Over the next three or four years, Archbold gained control of virtually all of the remaining oil-region refineries. In 1875, Rockefeller completed his control of all the major refining centers by buying West Virginia refineries, particularly one of his major rivals, J. N. Camden Co. of Parkersburg. Camden then bought up most of the other area refineries for Standard without announcing their ownership by Standard.

Using his new dominant position, Rockefeller could dictate terms to the railroad and did so, getting even more favorable rates for his shipments. Then pipelines began to threaten his stranglehold, but he countered by buying up existing lines and building his own. He soon controlled the movement of oil and found that even more profitable than refining. (T 158-72)

In 1878, the Bradford oilfield came in, and Standard Oil worked quickly to complete pipelines to the wells, but even it couldn't keep up with the production, and oil ran into the ground. Standard, though not to blame for the overproduction, took advantage of it to quote a purchase price 20% below prevailing prices and demanded immediate shipment. It also favored shipments to its own refineries. These practices led to strong protest in the oil region. Empire Oil and The Pennsylvania Railroad, which owned most of Empire, decided to challenge Standard by building a pipeline from Bradford to the Empire's seaboard refineries,

Empire having bought up many of the refineries not controlled by Standard.

Rockefeller threatened Tom Scott, the director of the railroad, but Scott refused to relent. So Rockefeller quit shipping oil by Pennsylvania Railroad. The loss in revenue forced Scott to fire workers, run longer trains, and led to a terrible rail strike with much railroad property destroyed. Ultimately, though the pipeline was successfully built, Scott gave in to Standard by buying up the remaining stock of Empire and then selling all of the oil holdings to Standard at bargain prices.

At the same time, Standard purchased Columbia Conduit Company and thus became the dominant petroleum mover to the Baltimore refineries. Next Standard gained control of the refineries in Baltimore. By the end of 1878, Standard Oil controlled nearly 90 percent of the oil refined in the United States. By 1879, Standard controlled almost the entire pipeline system of Western Pennsylvania. When the Tidewater Pipeline was under construction, threatening the monopoly of Standard, Rockefeller used every tactic possible to stop it short of the thuggery recommended by one of his employees. Rockefeller worked out a deal with Tidewater's head, Byron Benson, in which the two would be able to control prices for oil shipment. Standard would get 88.5 percent of the Pennsylvania pipeline business and Tidewater the remainder. Finally, Standard controlled the Pennsylvania oilfields.
(T 197-215)

For years, Standard Oil exercised a global monopoly. In the mid eighties, about 70 percent of American oil was shipped overseas. But Standard's monopoly was broken when oil was discovered at the Russian port of Baku on the Caspian Sea in the early 1870s. In 1873, Robert Nobel bought a refinery in Baku. Soon his family's Nobel Brothers Petroleum Producing Company was in control of efficient, well-managed refineries treating the cheap, plentiful Russian oil. The Nobel brothers built a pipeline to the Caspian Sea and built the first oil tanker. Soon cut-rate kerosene flooded Europe's markets undercutting Standard. Then in the mid eighties, a Frenchman, Baron Alphonse de Rothschild, had refineries constructed in Rijecko and Trieste on the Adriatic Sea. In 1891, Marcus Samuel began to market de Rothschild's kerosene in the far east. The next year, Marcus Samuel and Royal Dutch began marketing oil from Burma and Java. These two companies later merged as Shell Oil. Standard was able to keep the cheap Russian oil out of the U. S., but it no longer had its monopoly of the world markets. (T 243-9)

Various legal challenges came to Standard's dominance, but its attackers had little success in curtailing its railroad rebates or aggressive anticompetitive practices in marketing its kerosene. Standard chose never to get a perfect monopoly even as it sold more than 90 percent of all kerosene year after year and provided huge dividends to its stockholders. (T 258-60)

In the early eighties, Standard Oil owned only four producing properties, but the wells of Western Pennsylvania began to be depleted, and all of Standard's refineries and rail cars were in need of oil. Fortunately for Standard, large deposits of oil were discovered near Lima, Ohio in May 1885. The oil was not good, clean, paraffin-based oil like that of Pennsylvania. The Ohio oil provided less kerosene and had a high sulfur content that smelled horribly and corroded machinery. In spite of its low quality, Rockefeller decided to spend millions of dollars to buy oil properties and to build pipelines and storage facilities. He hired a chemist, Herman Frasch, to solve the problems in refining the oil and making a usable illuminant from it. By 1887, Frasch had discovered that by using copper oxide he could remove the sulfur, and in 1888, Frasch completed the process of cleaning the oil and making it a product that could be sold to the public. Following this success, Standard bought Union Oil and three other large producers before buying three hundred thousand acres of Pennsylvania and West Virginia oilfields (T283-6)

In the U. S. in the late 1890s, Pure Oil was Standard's only competitor, but the discovery of huge quantities of oil at the Spindletop salt dome outside of Beaumont, Texas in January 1901 changed all that. Standard's marketing subsidiary, Waters-Pierce had been thrown out of Texas for violations of Texas' antitrust laws, so Standard stood by while 500 companies were formed in the first year alone. Companies growing out of this oil boom were Gulf, Texaco, and Humble, now Exxon. Soon other major discoveries in Oklahoma, Kansas, Illinois, and California eliminated Standard's monopoly. (T430-1)

Chapter 9

Monopoly

In the fourth oil novel, *The Warners* (1901) by Gertrude Potter Daniels, a melodrama, the evil force is the oil trust, obviously Standard Oil. *The Warners* traces the life history of Cyrus Warner, a hard-working, lowly-paid drudge. He meets and marries the beautiful, loving, pure Betty. He is able to buy an oil well cheaply, one somewhere in the south. He and Betty move into a cottage near it, living happily and quietly off the income of the well. Little Betty is born and grows up to become a beautiful young lady like her mother. All is happiness until Anthony J. Fellows arrives in his private rail car. Fellows offers to buy the well. Cyrus says it is not for sale. Fellows implies that he will have it in time. The price of oil starts going down. Cyrus decides he will have to sell, so he goes back to see Fellows, taking Little Betty with him. Fellows offers Cyrus 1/3 of what Cyrus believes his well to be worth. Fellows doesn't care whether he buys or not, for as the narrator says, "by a word he sent down the price of oil. He didn't care. In the end he had to gain. Millions backed him, 100's his opponent." (*W* 108) But Cyrus refuses the offer, considering it unfairly low. Because Fellows controls the market, he knows that he will eventually be able to buy the well.

While Fellows is bargaining with Cyrus, his son, Teddy, is talking to Little Betty. Teddy is described as a "young man, very dark and very bestial in countenance." (*W* 109) He and Betty strike up a friendship. Little Betty, Betty, and Cyrus grow steadily more impoverished. Finally, Cyrus goes back to Anthony J. Fellows and offers to sell the well. Fellows says that he will think about it and let Cyrus know if he wants it. In time Fellows buys. Teddy meanwhile sweeps Little Betty off her feet. She becomes his mistress, and when he grows tired of her, he throws her out into the street. She returns to her family and is taken in. This increases the hate that Cyrus Warner feels toward the Fellows. Later he begins his way back when he strikes iron ore. Again, Fellows shows up to buy him out. He can stand it no longer. He learns from an anarchist friend how to make a bomb. He confronts Fellows in his home. He raises the bomb in preparation for throwing it at Fellows, but the book ends with this sentence: "And Cyrus looking directly into his enemy's eyes began to lower the bomb." (*W* 251) This is melodrama and not very good melodrama.

    Though Gertude Potter Daniels tries to show the evils of the oil trust, little here has anything to do with reality. How Cyrus managed to buy the well in the first place is unclear. If he paid what he could afford, he cheated Mr. Fisher as much as Fellows did him. There were no oilfields by a cottage all by itself. How the oil was marketed is not clear. A chief executive of a trust would not be out buying a single oil well, and he certainly wouldn't be influencing the price of oil in order to do so. Ironically, Daniels, rich daughter of a steel magnet[*], writes critically of the oil

---

[*]http://query.nytimes.com/gst/abstract.html?res=9E04E2DA153AE533A25753C2A96F9C94609ED7CF

trust and creates a character with part of John David Rockefeller's name, but she was unlikely to be very effective in her criticism of it with such a clumsy melodramatic vehicle as this. Yet she describes some of the ways Fellows dealt with Warner that are much like the way Ron Chernow describes Rockefeller using with his opponents — the calm assertive manner of Fellows seems to fit Rockefeller's manner. One chapter of the biography is entitled "Sphinx." In it Chernow speaks of Rockefeller's "imperturbable style."(*T* 108)

Chapter 10

An Early Ohio Oilfield Novel

The next oil novel, *Silenced by Gold* (1902) by Harry Rangeler, makes no mention of Standard or any other large producers even though it is set in Ohio where Standard dominated the production. Instead, the Ohio field seems to be wide open to small independent operators. The novel begins with the protagonist, young Charley Ford, already an experienced tool dresser, beginning work on a wildcat well not far from his home town. The well is being supervised by a rather self-important dandy, the son of the owner of the operation, Mr. Pankis. Charley is working on the day shift, here referred to as a day "tour," pronounced to rhyme with "sour." He assists the driller, Jack Norton, who is to become his long time good friend. There is even an opportunity for Charley to show off his manly form in reshaping and sharpening a bit using a sledge hammer. The local townspeople come to watch the drilling as a form of entertainment. One of the watchers is the young, beautiful, good, bright, well-educated, brash Mabel Gray. Immediately Charley is attracted to her. But so is handsome, crude John Pitts, tool dresser on the night tour. Pitts, an experienced lady's man, tells Charley that he will have Mabel Gray as his. Charley says nothing.

When Charley and John get their first pay, they go to a saloon. Then drunk, they go to a bawdy house. When Charley wakes up the next morning, he has a hangover and no money. He vows never to do this again and doesn't. Here we have the first example in literature of a common behavior of tool dressers, drillers, and roughnecks.

Charley discovers that one of the older men who comes to watch the drilling is his mother's brother, his Uncle Mike. His uncle owns the adjoining farm to the one on which Charley's crew is drilling. Mike hopes that if oil is struck, his land will become valuable, too. Charley meets his cousin, Henry, and they become fast friends although Charley thinks at first he is another rival for the affections of Mabel Gray. After much ado, Charley wins the affection of Mabel, but in so doing gains the enmity of John Pitts, a formidable adversary. John, enraged, pulls a gun on Charley and probably would have shot him if Jack Norton hadn't knocked the gun aside with a thrown tool.

The love triangle affects the well drilling. For revenge and for some other deceptive purpose involving young Pankis, Pitts cuts almost all the way through the drill string just before turning over the operation to Jack and Charley. After they start drilling, the drill string breaks off and falls into the hole. For some reason, we are supposed to believe that the supervisors will think Jack and Charley did it. Jack and Charley know John Pitts did it, but they have no proof. The sabotage ruins the well because the string cannot be fished out. The decision is made to abandon the lease, and thus Uncle Mike's hope of wealth is lost along with all the jobs of the crew. Mabel and Charley decide that he will go away to work until they can make enough money to get married.

Charley goes to work in a pump station, working

there for three years and saving his money, but the bank in which he has his money fails, and he loses it all. While working at the pump station, he has an opportunity to be a hero. Near where he is working, they are shooting a well with 250 quarts of nitroglycerin. When it is exploded, rocks and water are thrown up. Then gas comes out and explodes. A man is on the top of the derrick at the time. Charley recognizes that the man is John Pitts. Charley sees that he can help John escape from the flames. Though Pitts has been his enemy, Charley endangers his life to rescue him. Charley's arm is wounded, but Pitts is near death. Charley still goes near the flames to pull six more men out. Before John dies, he confesses to Charley that he had cut the drill string at Pankis' instruction.

Charley recovers from his injuries and goes back to work at the pump station. He uses his free time to study and becomes well-educated. His old friend Jack Norton has become an independent contractor. He offers Charley a job as a tool dresser. He soon becomes a driller, then saves his money, and becomes a partner with Jack. He is doing well and corresponding with Mabel, and they plan for their wedding. But disaster strikes in the form of a wind storm. The derrick begins to blow over. Charley runs and just avoids being hit, but one of his men is killed when the crown block hits him. Charley's rig is completely destroyed, and he is once more penniless. He, in despair, writes Mabel giving up all hope of their being together. Uncle Mike sells the farm, and Mabel moves to Illinois with the family.

A rich oil man for whom Charley drilled wells, Mr. Corning, loans Charley money to repair his machinery, and Charley gets back in the drilling business. Two wells later, Charley pays him off. Four wells later, Charley becomes a full partner with Jack again. Then he buys back his Uncle's farm, and Corning leases it from him and pays him to drill the wells. Charley strikes oil there. He goes to find Mabel. He doesn't tell her of his new wealth. She is now willing to marry him even if he is penniless. They marry and move back to the old farm bringing his sick Uncle Mike with them. There is a joyous reunion at the old farm, and we are to assume they will live happily thereafter.

This is as close to a generic oilfield novel as one can get, the first of its kind, having many of the characteristic elements to be seen in later oil novels — the romantic love, the protagonist who stoically persists in spite of adversities to attain his goal, an adversary who is physically imposing and threatening, and a friend made on the job who remains loyal through many hardships.

Chapter 11

Refining Rivals

With Francis Newton Thorpe's novel *Divining Rod* (1905), the monopolistic practices of Standard Oil come to the fore again, but this time the practices are not that of Standard, but that of a single large producer/refiner in the Pennsylvania field. Thorpe* writes as if there is no such thing as Standard Oil. But the practice of controlling refining techniques and getting rebates is central to the plot. The story is much more complex than that summary might imply.

The novel begins with a poor farmer's daughter, Helen, lying on a hillside in Western Pennsylvania enjoying a summer's day. Soon her reverie is interrupted by the arrival of her father, Thomas Bostwick, and Elder Blaisdon. Elder Blaisdon, a local mystic in an off-shoot of the Methodist congregation, has a divining rod in his hand. He follows it right to where she is lying. There is where the oil well will be drilled. But before the well can be drilled, her father agrees to sell part of his land to a shrewd gentleman, John C. Webster. They soon strike an abundance of oil. They apparently control most of the production in the whole country, right there in that little valley. They build refineries. They work on improving techniques of refining. They become bitter rivals. One day Helen

---

*Thorpe, 1857-1927, was a Professor of American Constitutional History at the University of Pennsylvania and author of a biography of Benjamin Franklin and several books on the American Constitution.

falls from a tree and Percy Webster, John Webster's son, gives her and her father a ride to the doctor. So he escapes the enmity which Bostwick holds toward his father.

Helen goes off to school and becomes a lady. Meanwhile, Webster's company becomes The People's Oil Company and grows increasingly more powerful, particularly because of the machinations of one Amos Gilfern, Webster's chief assistant. Amos is paying Elder Blaisdon, now a trusted employee of Bostwick, to spy on his boss, and Blaisdon even sets fire to one of Bostwick's refineries. People's Oil also has the benefit of a patent developed by one of its employees, Kenneth Forbes. Percy Webster has stolen the patent from Forbes and recorded it in his own name.

Helen Bostwick returns from school to a beautiful new home and finds her father in difficult circumstances because of the financial pressure brought to bear by Webster and Gilfern. Bostwick turns to his daughter for help. He explains his problems with the rail rebates to People's Oil. She seems to understand his problems well, and he hires her as confidential clerk

While making the rounds of her father's holding, she observes an explosion on one of Webster's' nearby wells of Webster's. A man has been badly injured and is lying on the ground unconscious. No one seems to be doing anything for him. The boss, young Percy Webster, comes up and, without looking at the wounded man, says "I guess it's all over with the fellow." He also says that his workers are all reckless and won't follow instructions. Helen insists that someone send for a doctor. They realize that the injured man is Forbes, the man who developed the refining patent. Percy still seems to have no concern about the welfare of one of his workmen. The doctor arrives and discovers Forbes is still alive. There are no hospitals. One of Forbes's friends agrees to take off from work without pay to nurse him. While Forbes is sick, Helen sends books to him. One is a book of sermons, the other a book of chemistry. From this experience, Helen decides the town needs a hospital and takes it on herself to raise the money for one. Forbes gets well, but because he can no longer do the rough field work, he is fired by Webster. The doctor recommends him to Helen and Thomas Bostwick, and they hire him to replace Blaisdon.

Amos Gilfern buys a lease out from under Webster and then sells it back to him for a million dollars. With this money, he buys into a partnership with Bostwick. Forbes provides them a new and improved patent which produces even better kerosene, giving them a competitive edge over People's Oil.

Webster and Forbes both pursue Helen. She seems to favor Forbes. But there is a young woman, Jennie Stinson, with an illegitimate child. Elder Blaisdon lies to Helen, telling her the child is Forbes'. In reality, it is Percy Webster's. Elder Blaisdon uses the divining rod again, and it selects Percy, "by the will of heaven her destined husband." So Helen agrees to marry Percy and is in the act of doing so when there is a horrendous refinery fire. In the ensuing scene, Percy is seriously injured. Thinking he is dying, he confesses that he is the father of Jennie's child. Then Helen realizes how unfair she has been to Forbes and feels great guilt.

Following the fire, the Bostwick oil empire is in danger of being swallowed up by Webster. While being financially threatened by Webster, Bostwick has a heart attack and dies.

After Bostwick dies, we have a marriage of love and oil. Forbes provides his patents and his money to rescue the company: "Let us fight the enemy side by side, Helen. At least justice is with us, and I believe that justice will triumph; it shall triumph; we will learn how to conquer." (DR 355-6) As over-written as this is, it is still interesting how the oil business and romantic love blend.

Chapter 12

In Defense of Standard

With our next novel, *Oil Well In the Woods* (1905), we find a defender of Standard Oil, its author, John Christopher O'Day. He had been a scout for Standard and as a result had grown wealthy from investing in a well that came in as a gusher.* O'Day thinks he is writing the first novel about oil. And he sets out in his introduction to show what is factual, what fictional:

> The following story is based upon Oil Country events, with which many of my readers may find themselves familiar.
>
> It has been the aim of the writer to appeal to those who live within the confines of oildom, but at the same time he has endeavored to portray characters and plot in such a manner that the tale may interest all lovers of fiction.
>
> Where consistent, he has retained the names of those genial fellows who rightfully belong to any scheme with which crude-oil is associated, or further anything pertaining to the history of the Oil Industry.
>
> Weatherbee, the villain of the plot, while purely a fictional character, is not an overdrawn picture of the "smooth gentleman" who, from Pit Hole to Bradford, was always on hand with a "good thing."

---

*O'Day went on to a stellar career as a medical doctor, developing two important surgical techniques, one still bearing his name, O'Day's damper gastrojejunostomy.

Facts have been adhered to, decorated of course with fictional ornaments, in the hope of securing for this book a place among that class of works known as "Historical Novels."

The terrible death which befell so many drillers during the early days of the oil business, before the secrets of mother earth had been learned, is described realistically in the burning of the "Nelly."

The opening of Triumph Hill, the rise and fall of early oil towns, the Bradford boom, the McKean County fire, the "646" gusher, and the panic which followed its development, the intimidating and shut-down movements, the discovery of oil in Ohio, and the awful fire and flood of 1892, are events of which any one would make a book of no little interest. (*OWW* iii, iv)

The hero of the story, John Payne, is a child as the story begins. His father is working on a well being drilled by Mr. Weatherbee. The well is on the property of Mrs. Martin, the widow of a civil-war hero. Weatherbee has written the lease agreement with Mrs. Martin so that he will retain the rights to the oil on her land if a well is drilled and no oil is found. So he conspires to stop drilling before reaching the depth at which oil should be found. John and his beloved playmate, Nina Smedley, overhear Weatherbee's plotting, and he tells his father. His father works with the driller to foil the plot by drilling deeper than they were told. Unfortunately, the well comes in with gas and catches on fire, killing his father. Weatherbee still manages to steal the well from the widow.

John's mother takes in wash to support John and

herself, and he sells papers. The father of his friend, Nina, becomes rich and moves his family to Oil City.

John grows up, going through a dare-devil adolescent period before settling down to become a driller. He then buys several rigs and is on his way to some economic success when he is invited to a Christmas party. There he sees Nina but doesn't recognize her. But he falls in love with her after only the short acquaintance and remains so for years. He wants to see her again but is called away on business. He leaves a letter saying that she should write him if he will be allowed to see her. Nina has been impressed with him and wants to see him. She hasn't recognized him either. She mistakenly shows the letter to her father. Her father is a foolish man, who wants someone for his daughter who has money and can provide her a lifestyle similar to the one to which she has become accustomed. He orders her not to see John because John is just a driller.

Grace Weatherbee is Nina's best friend, and she wants Nina to marry her brother, George. He gambles in the oil market and loses. He forges checks. He doesn't care for Nina but decides that he wants to marry her because of her wealth. His father thinks that George might reform if he marries Nina. Nina strongly dislikes George, but since she is a good Victorian daughter, she follows her father's wishes in the matter. John hears of the marriage and despairs.

Meanwhile, Mr. Weatherbee has been scheming to get all the wealth of Mr. Smedley. By bribing someone to let him scout a well, Weatherbee learns that a great discovery has been made, one which will send the price of oil down. He sells his oil while the price is still high, but he doesn't tell Smedley, who has followed his advice in investing. Smedley loses everything and dies of a heart attack when he is shocked by the news.

Nina, in the midst of an unhappy honeymoon cruise to Europe, finds out and returns. She discovers her financial state, and it is as bad as her marital state. George has struck her on two occasions. When he attempts to a third time, she protects herself with a pistol. She leaves immediately, taking nothing and having no money. She wanders the street and decides to see if one of her former servants will take her in. She goes to the servant's house and is welcomed there. The woman has two children and works out of the house. Nina makes herself useful by tending the children and keeping house.

No one knows what has happened to her. People think she has drowned. But she does send a note to an old family friend, Mr. Graham, telling him that she is safe and with friends. Ten years pass. John still loves Nina but assumes she is still married to George and makes no attempt to locate her. He buys into some producing wells cheaply when others rush off to a new oilfield. The other field runs out of oil quickly, but he reworks and torpedoes some of the old wells and gets good production. Then he buys leases in Ohio and starts to drill there.

Mr. Weatherbee has tried to buck Standard Oil and gone broke. John finds out that Weatherbee still holds the lease on property adjoining his in Ohio. He comes to Oil City and buys the lease. While there, he tries to locate Nina. A hotel clerk tells him about her disappearance, about the note Mr. Graham received and about George's remarriage to a "floozy" who has taken what money he hasn't wasted. John has no way to locate Nina, but while he is in Oil City, there is a great storm, and the city is flooded. He tries to rescue people, and while doing so, he notices that one of the people he is rescuing is Nina. Then an even biggerdisaster occurs. The contents of the oil tanks above the city overflow, and a passing train catches the oil on fire, causing most of the city to go up in flames. Mr. Weatherbee is one of the victims. But John succeeds in saving himself, Nina, her friend, and her friend's family. He takes them to his mother's house in Bradford where they are made welcome. He buys the old Smedley home, which has been vacant. Then he proposes to Nina, and she accepts. The reader may, of course, wonder what she has been doing for the last ten years. Obviously, the author wanted to get in the great Oil City fire and flood, so he had to have ten years pass in order to keep historical accuracy, since he had described the McLean fire earlier.

In addition to giving us the story of the romance of John and Nina, O'Day frequently launches into essays and notes to support the benefits that Standard Oil provided for oil people:

> Ten years had passed since the rise and fall of that never-to-be-forgotten place of wild stampeding and blasted fortunes, Cherry Grove.
> The oil industry was a youth no longer; the wild oats, as well as the wild-cats, had given way to the

wiser judgment of maturity, and the business assumed a better and more substantial trend.

After a hard fought battle, the Standard succeeded in getting control of the oil market and proclaimed through their agent, Joseph Seep, that the price of oil would be governed by the natural law of supply and demand, instead of the uncertain Door of the Exchange.

The brokers tried hard to have this, their death blow, reconsidered; but Standard Oil, acting for a common good, paid no attention to their protests; the Exchange, with its record of broken homes and pauperized producers, had to go.

With the exception of a very few who played on the inside, no one made money on "wind oil," and many sighs of relief were given when, for a certainty, it was known that buying oil on margin was a thing of the past. (OWW 312)

O'Day also managed to work his support for Standard into the plot. The villain gets his just deserts at the hands of Standard supposedly because of his methods. When John inquires about Weatherbee, he learns of how Weatherbee lost his money.

> "Don't see much of him around since he went defunct," he added; "the fellow hasn't a friend in the town."
>
> "I am unable to imagine Weatherbee a bankrupt," I replied. "He was an exceedingly shrewd business man."
>
> "Wasn't shrewd enough to buck Standard Oil, though."
>
> "I didn't hear any of the particulars."
>
> "Well, there isn't much to it," he went on;

"Weatherbee began under-selling the Standard at Philadelphia and New York; his scheme was to have them call a halt, and take him and his plant into the 'trust.'

"It wasn't long, however, till he found other oils coming in at a price way below his, and of course people bought where they could buy the cheapest; so Weatherbee, to sell his oil, had to come down to the lowest price.

"Finding this wouldn't do, he shifted to Baltimore, Chicago and Cleveland, and placed his oil on the market of these cities on a par with other oil.

"There was no land talk or fuss, but strange enough, refined oil went up again in Philadelphia and New York, and fell in Baltimore, Chicago and Cleveland.

"He then tried to worm an under-test oil into these cities that he might compete with the unseen enemy, but this was the first symptom of the man losing his head.

"The explosion of a lamp, killing a woman and her child, led to an investigation, and the dealer who was handling the Weatherbee Oil was closed up by the Government. . . . It was his methods not his business which aroused the spirit of antagonism in the Standard." (OWW317-8)

If one reads this defense of Standard Oil carefully, it is easy to see how Standard could force out any opposition — not just villainous ones, and the railroad rebates aren't even touched on here. O'Day even has pictures of and lists of the local independent refiners in an effort to refute the charge that Standard monopolized the industry. Chernow reports in his biography of Rockefeller that by 1877, Standard oil controlled 90% of the oil refined in the United States: "Perhaps a hundred tiny refineries still eked out a meager living in the interstices of the industry, but they were mostly tolerated as minor nuisances and scarcely threatened Standard oil." *(T 204)*

Chapter 13

Shooter Shot

Standard Oil is again the enemy in the next oil novel, *The Spotter*, by William Canfield*, published in 1907. In it, Standard is called Cygnet Oil Producing and Refining Company, and Rockefeller is called Mr. Lanphere. According to Chernow, Rockefeller lived in Cleveland, and later New York, and only visited the Pennsylvania oil territory once. But in this novel, Mr. Lanphere operates his great oil empire from one of the oil boom towns. He takes an active part in stealing oil land from our hero, Duncan Cameron. Cameron is a successful farmer, who owes nothing on his farm and has money in the bank. His neighbors have all sold or leased their land and are rich. Cameron sees them all waste their money and sees that they are less happy than when they were less rich, so he does not wish to sell his land. But he has difficulty not doing so. Scouts are continually after him to sell or lease. People cross his land and destroy his crops and trees. He still says no. And he makes statements about the unfair practices of Cygnet and Lanphere.

The narrator describes Lanphere as "a smooth-shaven, soft-speaking, pious fraud." (S 45) He attended church and carried "his Sunday air at all times." But when he hears what Cameron says about him, he

---

*Canfield (1855-1937) is best known for his novel, The Legends of the Iroquois, which was released in a new edition in 2002.

Cover image of *The Spotter*

102   Fountain Wells

strikes the desk with a clenched fist and says, "Damn the Scotch Meddler." He says he will bring him to his terms, and he soon comes up with a scheme to do it. He uses his employee Ira Wheeler to approach Cameron. Wheeler says that he is signing up independents to form a company to oppose Cygnet. Cameron agrees and puts everything he has into a business with Wheeler. It loses everything and is taken over by Lanphere and Cygnet. Wheeler marries the daughter of Tubbs, Cameron's neighbor. Tubbs was unhappy with his wealth and had invested with Wheeler even though he didn't trust him. He is unhappy that his daughter has thrown in with the scoundrel. Wheeler, to avoid prosecution and Cameron's revenge, leaves for Paris with his new bride.

Much of the middle part of the novel is not about oil. Instead, it concerns, Mrs. Wheeler, her gradual maturity, and final escape from Wheeler. Wheeler is conned by members of a commune, Citizen Lefevre and LeGarde. Cameron follows Wheeler's trail and after two years catches up with him. When he attacks Wheeler, Citizen Lefevre hits Cameron behind the head. Wheeler asks the citizens to take Cameron away and kill him. They accept but don't do it. Instead, they blackmail Wheeler. Ultimately, Cameron has amnesia and can't remember anything since his childhood. He is allowed to return to Scotland. Wheeler loses all his money to the members of the commune and bums a ride on a Cygnet boat back to America. Mrs. Wheeler, having earlier escaped from Wheeler, is rescued by some of her oil rich neighbors who are vacationing in Paris. The neighbors and she go to Scotland, get

Chapter 13   103

Cameron out of his amnesia, and return to the United States with him. There, he supervises an oilfield. One day while working, he meets Tubbs' son, Coon, who had disappeared. Coon is a better man without the money he had wasted. He is a moonshiner, an unregistered torpedoer like Tickly-Bender in *The Devil's Hat*. He is being pursued by a spotter. Similar to a bounty hunter, a spotter works for the company who holds the torpedo patent in order to prevent companies from buying the service of moonshiners. The spotter who is after Coon is Wheeler, their old enemy. While Coon is talking to Cameron, Wheeler shoots Coon from cover. Cameron works on Coon's wound and keeps him from bleeding to death, leaving himself open to being shot. Other people come up, and Wheeler escapesl.

Coon heals and plans to do no more moonshining but needs to make one more trip to a cave in order to transfer the nitroglycerin to a friend as he explains to his sister:

> We moonshiners had to pack our glycerine on our backs, and we had a habit of hiding it in certain places near wells that we expected to shoot, or in any good territory. Sometimes we would make a good many trips and get a whole lot of the nitro stored up, and then some blamed spotter would catch on and capture the supply. Another chap and I found a cave up here in the city a-ways, and when we had some money we put in a big supply, for it is in a mighty safe place. Just a few days before I was shot, my chum was pinched when shooting a well over near Custer City, and of course they railroaded him to the penitentiary for two years and a half.

"Now, you see, Bet, I'm going out of the moonshine business, but I don't want to leave the nitro up there in the rocks. In time, some excursion party might run onto it, get to fooling with the cans, and then there'd be trouble for innocent people. I've written to a couple of the boys in the profession telling them where they can find it and promising to mark the spot for them. (S 303)

He goes to the cave and is confronted by Wheeler. In the struggle that ensues, the nitroglycerin explodes. Only fragments of the two are found, but in the fragments are papers which show the connection between Lanphere and Wheeler. Cameron's lawyer now has a case against Lanphere and Cygnet. Lanphere settles out of court, and Cameron has more than enough money to buy himself another farm far away from any oilfield.

Chapter 14

Law and Oil

The villain of the next oil novel is not a monopolist but a greedy farmer. Thirty chapters, 292 pages, of *Tract Number 3377* (1907) had been completed when the author, George H. Higgins, died in 1905. His sister, Margaret Haffey, picked up the project and wrote the final 92 pages, little of which has to do with the oil business. Just as O'Day provided an explanation of the factual items in his novel, so does Haffey in her preface:

> Although we call this narrative a romance, we do not wish to convey to the reader the idea that it is simply fiction; for, in fact, the incidents herein related are more of them truths — slightly embellished perhaps — than pictures from an imaginative brain. While it might not be called historical, it is in many instances true to the life of that particular time and place, told by one who entered the Bradford Oilfield a young man, inexperienced in that kind of work but with a quick eye and true sense of humor; one who worked that he might obtain the means to continue his law study, and who succeeded, as his associates who knew him as a successful lawyer in the Courts of Pennsylvania will attest. (*TN 3377* Preface)

The line about sense of humor is quite relevant, for this book has more funny characters and scenes in it than any other oil novel. Most of the humor involves the older members of two farm families of Western Pennsylvania. The novel begins with the chief of these, the Underwoods. Seldom do these people go to town, but Enoch, called Een, has to go into to town for supplies. He discovers that everything has changed there because oil has been discovered. Though very provincial and uneducated, Een has a lot of horse sense as he shows when he tells his family about his trip to town. I am quoting a long passage because it tells about the boom in oil, it shows Een's character — one of the best in oilfield fiction — and it is funny:

> Een replied, "I've got so gol durned much t' tell, I don't know heow tu begin."
> "Begin et th' fust, 'n course," said Mandy.
> "Yas, s'pose thet's th' way. Yer see; th' roads wuz all-fired muddy, so when I got deown tu th' road thet Dave Jenkins hauled logs eout'n tu years ergo, I jest made up my mind I'd tek thet, 'n et' ud bring me eout onter th' Tuna road 'bove Tarport; yer know, Josh, thet es th' road I show'd yer, when yer cum 'nd helped me drag thet big buck in, that I killed year ago this spring." Josh nodded. "Wall, yer see thet road crosses th' run 'n' goes erlong on th' side hill — er ruther on th' bench erbove th' creek. Wal, zi wuz sayin', I got t' thet road, un thinks I t' myself, thet 's th' best way, un 'll save lots uv mud. So I jes' sez, Haw! Bright, Haw! Red, 'n' turned up tlet road. Wal, I didn't see ner hear nuthin' strange till I got deown purty nigh Tuna road; jest erbout a hundred rods 'fore ye' git thar, ye' go up a little rise uv greound, 'n' yer kin see deown th' valley three or four miles, kin jes' see right over th' trees un likes; ye' kin see th' blacksmith shop 'n' meetin' house et

"Here ole man, I'll gin it to you first." from *Tract Number 3377*.

Tarport. Wal, when I look't deown th' valley I just sed, 'Whoa', un set thar 'n' look't fer full five minutes; then I sed t' myself, 'Wal, I'll be gol durned!' "

"What was 't?" ejaculated Mandy, impatiently.

"Aint I tellin' yer 's fast zi kin? Fust I seen new lumber piled all over, lots uv new bildin's, houses 'n' sich in Tarport, 'n' a hull lot uv high things bilt up suthin' like ladders standin' up, 'n' cumin' purty nigh t'gether et th' top, with braces runin' deown each way; big wood'n wheels et th' bottom, un a leetle wheel clean on top ; seemed t' me th' wuz seventy-five' tu a hundred feet high; then they had ropes 'n' iron bars; 'n' men 'n' teams seemed t' fill purty nigh all th' roads. Thar wuz a lot uv big tubs, tu. I called 'em tubs, but sum un tole me they wuz tanks; 'n' kinder a funny smell, un arter 'bout fifteen minutes I jest sed t' myself, 'Een, I'll bet seven leetle devils 'et yer rich.' Yer see I jes' know'd 'et they'd struck ile."

"But, Dad," interrupted Josh.

"Never yeou mind," said Mandy, now more interested than ever; "yer go on, Een."

"Wa-al, ya-as, I did go on, when I kinder got my breath, 'til I got purty nigh th' main road, when I seen thet th' road wuz all block'd 'ith a big biler 'et he'd got tipped over. I druv deown nigh es I could, un th' wuz half a dozen men, 'n' tu teams, un th' men wuz lickin' 'n' swearin' 'n' liftin', but the' couldn't budge et. I sed, 'Hullo! fellers, what's up?' Wal, I'll not tell yer what the' sed, — thet es, all the' sed, — but when one uv 'em who wuz boss, seen my team uv oxen, he sed, 'Say, stranger, I'm d—d glad yer cum; neow 'f yer'll jes' hitch thet thar team uv yeourn on ahead uv these hosses, 'n' git this 'ere biler rolled back onter th' trucks, 'n' help us up thet thar hill, I'll gin yer ten dollars.' 'Yer don't mean it,' sed I. 'Yes, by ——, I du,' sed he. But I jes' stood 'n' look't et' im, un I guess he know'd thet I wuz thinkin'—'Don't b'leve yer got thet much munny,' fer 'e sed, 'Here, ole man, I'll gin et t' yer fust,' un I'll be gol durned ef he didn't pull eout uv his trouser pockit a roll uv bills bigger'n my arm; tens, twentys, 'n' I guess hundreds, but didn't see none big es thet, un gin me th' ten dollars right thar."

"Whar's them ten dollars?" broke in Mandy, growing more and more interested.

"Never mind thet neow,—yer jes' wait 'till I git through 'ith my story, will yer? Wal, I tuk thet ten, 'n' tuk eout my leathern wallet, 'n' undone et, 'n' put et erway, 'n' thet thar chap jes' stood 'n' grinned t' see me. Wal, I onhitch'd frum th' wagin, 'n' hitch'd on es he sed, 'n' 'n less then 'n hour we had th' hull thing dun. Then I sed, 'Look a here, Mister, neow we'v' got thet dun, tell me what yer goin' ter du with thet big biler, 'n' tell me what in th' Ole Harry hez broke luse in here?' He sed, "Say! whar d' yean live?' 'Up Tram Holler,' sez I, , 'bout er dozen miles er more! 'Wal,' he sed, 'didn't yer know thet they'd struck ile here on th' creek?' 'No,' sez I, 'have the'? 'n' whar be yeou goin' with thet biler?' 'Gain' t' drill a well on Lige Peters' farm,' 'Drill a well!' sez I, 'why, he's got a spring! what does he want uv a well?' 'Oh, be yer dum? an ile well,' sed he. 'I guess I be dum,' sez I, 'n' I guess Mandy 'n' th' younguns 'll be dum tu when I tell 'em.'

"Wal, I hitch'd th' oxen back onter th' wagin 'n' started agin, 'n' I jes' kept meetin' teams, 'n' wagins, 'n' men, 'n' ev'ry one seemed t' be hustlin' fer fear sum un 'uld git thar fust, 'n' jes' turnin' eoout fer teams, 'n'llookin' reound t' see what wuz goin' on, I didn't git t' th' grocery' til' tu o'clock. Come nigh 'gitt'n run over mor'n a dozen times, tu. Wal, I got up t' th' las' bridge, jes' afore yer turn t' go up t' th' store, 'n' es I druv over 'n' turned, thar was mor'n twenty stores ; — hardware stores, grocery stores, clothin' stores 'n' s'lunes." "What," said Mandy, "whar the' sell whiskey? Een Underwood, tell me, did you go inter one uv them thar places?" "Wal, Mandy, 'twas like this, yer see; neow don't git yer narves t' wobblin'; jes' yer wait 'til I tell yer. Wal, I wuz drivin' 'long, 'n' a feller wuz stuck right in th' road 'n front uv er s'lune, 'n' I hitch'd on ahead 'n' pull'd 'im eout, 'n' he sed, 'here, pard, here's tu dollars, 'n' cum in 'ith me.' I didn't know what he wanted, so uv course I went in, 'n' he throw'd fifty cents deown on th' counter, 'n' sez he, 'what'll ye' hev?' 'N' I sez, 'I dunno.' 'N' he sez, 'gin us sum uv thet thar rockenrye;' so I jes' drink't sum uv thet."

"Wal," said Mandy, drawing a sigh of relief, "et's bad enuff gain' in sich a place, but uv course yean didn't know what et wuz und ef yer had ever a drink't eny uv thet thar whiskey, I never c'd uv fergin ye' es long es ye' lived. But then I know'd yer wouldn't du sich a thing. But say, whar es thet thar munny?"

"N eow never mind 'bout thet yit. Wal, I druv t' th' grocery, und I'll be gol durned ef I know'd th' place; — bilt twict es big, 'n' piled full uv stuff, 'n' a dozen clerks 'n' fellers a waitin' on folks. I fin'ly got t' see a feller long 'nuff ter' tell 'im what I wanted, 'n' ast 'im whar Olson wuz. 'He's eout'n th' back yard seein' th' well flow,' sez he. 'Yeou kin go eout thar while I'm a ti'n' yer goods up,' sez he. Un I went.

Th' ile wuz jes' a gushin' eout'n a pipe inter a tank, the' called et, 'n' Olson sed, 'Een Underwood, d' yer know 'et thet thar ile well's o flowin' tu hundred bar'ls uv ile a day, 'n' et's wuth tu dollars 'n' fifty cents a bar'l?' Un I sed, 'No! yer don't tell me?' 'Yas, I du,' sez he. Then I stood up 'n' look't et thet thar ile a pourin' inter thet thar tank 'til th' feller sed, 'Here's yer goods; seven dollars 'n' eighty cents.' So I went in 'n paid 'im." "Un fergot th' ile," said Mandy. Een appeared not to notice the interruption. "Wal, I can't tell yer much more t'night," said Een, " 'cept I stopp'd t' tu er three places whar the' wuz borin' fer ile. I ast a lot er questions, un guess the' tho't I wuz green, 'n' tried t' stuff me. One feller sed, when I ast 'im what them big wood'n wheels wuz, 'Them's bull-wheels.' I didn't say nuthin' but I jes' kinder look't ziff, mebby I b'leved et 'n' mebby I didn't. Et ernuther place whar I stopp'd, the' wuz pullin' th' big rope eout'n th' hole the'd made in th' greound; guess et wuz mor'n five hundred feet deep, un I sed, "What yer doin'?" Un th' feller sed, "Oh, diggin' a hole 'n th' greound." 'What fer?' sez I. 'When we git a leetle deeper,' sez he, 'we're goin' t' pull et eout un cut et up fer post holes, un sell 'em t' th' farmers t' set their fence posts in.' I sed, 'Ya—as! I'd like t' git 'bout a hundred,—but, say,' I sez, "uld the' be likely t' git dry, un shrink up so the'd be tu small 'fore a feller c'd git 'em set?' I jes' tho't I'd let 'im know I watn't no fule; but I didn't stay thar no longer. Jes' es I wuz a gitt'n inter th' wagin again, a feller 'ith rubber boots clean up ter his body, 'n' spurs on his boots, cum ridin' up et a gallup, 'n' he 'n' his hoss all kivered 'ith mud, un he sez, 'Say, be yean Mr. Underwood?' I sez, 'I be, 'n' who be yeou?' 'I'm Mr.

McKnight,' sez he, 'un I'm tole ye' got sum lan' erbout here, un I want tel' lease et fer ile.' I sed, 'No, I aint got none 'reound here,' un druy on. I didn't want no more uv them thar smart fellers tryin' t' fule me. But th' tell me thet Bill Mason, Al Summers, Sandy Ketchum, 'n' all them fellers 'long th' run, hev jes' got rich."

The clock struck twelve and Enoch said, "Ye-oll younguns git up sta'rs t' bed neow, mebby sum mornin' ye'll wake up t' fin' thet yer dad hez struck ile tu."

As they started for bed, Mandy said, "Let's see them twelve dollars." (TN37776-11)

The speech of the older Underwoods and of their neighbors, the Jenkins, is always rendered in the fashion seen here. The speech of their better educated children is written in standard English.

Then the plot shifts to Philadelphia, where Ashton Walbridge, our young hero, has just graduated from Allegheny College. He and his parents are in a carriage accident. He has minor injuries, but his father is killed, and his mother, because of a head injury, is unable to recognize anyone. His father had been quite wealthy, but Charles Metzgar, his trusted secretary, takes almost all of the money and runs away, leaving Ashton with only the house. Ashton mortgages it and uses the interest he receives to pay for his mother's care. He rents the house and heads for the oilfield to make some money. He gets a job on a well-drilling crew working on the Jenkins' farm. He becomes a roomer and boarder with the Underwoods, the Jenkins' neighbors. Their daughter Anna is away at school. Soon he and the Underwoods are fast friends.

Then, oddly enough, he receives a letter from his lawyer containing a title to a tract of land, the tract 3377 of the novel's title. It adjoins the Underwood's and Jenkins' farms and is land his father had received in payment of a debt. But the taxes had not been paid in the last four years. He finds out that the neighbor, David Jenkins, had bought the place for the $75 dollars in taxes owed on it. He and Een go to Smethport to see a lawyer about whether or not Ashton still has a claim on the land. The author is a lawyer, and it seems appropriate for the major question of the novel to be a legal one. Een has information about Jenkins' cutting timber from the tract and building skidways. Een's intelligent explanation of Jenkins behavior leads the lawyer to believe that Ashton has a good claim on the land, one which a jury will support. The lawyer advises Ashton to move on the land immediately. He does so, but before leaving Smethport, he meets Ann Underwood, and falls in love with her.

The crew on Jenkins' place has finished the well but will not let anyone near it, even the crew and landowner. It has been capped and made a "mystery" well. So Ashton has time to work with Een in building a shanty on his land. He sleeps outside there one night and is attacked by a cougar. He kills it with an ax. At almost the same time, the well blows the cap off and begins gushing. Ashton discovers that Jenkins has leased 100 acres of his tract to a contractor, Jim McKnight.

Ashton and Underwood decide to lease and sell part of their land to James Potts in order for Potts to

"It was laughable to see poor Jennings trying to protect his trees." from *Tract Number 3377*

Chapter 14   115

keep McKnight out. Potts begins setting up to drill. Jenkins, seeing the people cutting down trees, thinks that it is the crew of McKnight, so he comes over to help out by getting a boiler unstuck and by unloading lumber from a truck. He is enraged when he discovers that he has been deceived and that there is another claim to the land.

In these scenes following the striking of oil on his land, Dave Jenkins is a comic figure. He rushes about trying to stop the invasion of all of the boomers who are building a new town on his land. They cut down his fruit trees and tear down his fences. He stutters, and no one will listen until he finishes anything because they are in such a rush to get into the race for oil. He is also hen-pecked. There are numerous scenes where he seeks to avoid the wrath of Big Prue, his domineering wife. Finally he brings from town ten fifty-dollar bills, the first of their oil money. Then Big Prue forgives him.

McKnight tries to get Potts off the land by force, but Potts has hired 100 men. Violence is avoided and the date for a court trial is set. The trial comes down to a question of the honesty of David Jenkins. The attorney for Jenkins asks Een if he knows anything about Jenkin's reputation for truth and veracity. He said he didn't know anything about it, so the attorney thinks he has a good witness and pursues the questioning, but Een outwits him. The attorney insists that Een has contradicted himself:

> "I sed I didn't know nuthin' erbourt 'is repitashun fer truth 'n' veracity, but nobuddy didn't ast er-

"Yer Mystery's eout tekin' the' mornin' air, eh?" from *Tract Number 3377*

bout 'is repitashun fer lyin'. Ef thet es what yer want ter know erbout, I kin tell yer that Dave Jenkins hez got th' best repitashun fer bein' a liar uv eny man in McKean County thet I know."

"How do you know that?" asked the attorney excitedly."

"Wal, over eour way ef enybuddy's a tellin' a purty big story, yer allers hear sum one say 'thet feller es purty nigh as big a liar es Dave Jenkins', but yer never hear enybuddy called as big er liar es Dave es." (TN3777 218-9)

Thanks partially to Een's testimony, the jury finds in favor of Ashton. But tragedy is literally just around the corner. The Jenkins and Ashton are aboard a narrow-gauge train on the way home from the trial when the train comes around the corner and comes face to face with another oil country danger:

> Not more than ten minutes before the ill-fated train reached that spot, a large oil tank, standing on the hillside above the track, had burst and more than a thousand barrels of fresh crude oil flowed down onto and across the tracks of the railroad. The ditches of the road, as well as the roadbed itself, were filled for a distance of about thirty rods. (TN3777 234)

A spark from the train ignites the oil, and there is an explosion. Ashton is injured but manages to jump from the train to safety. He goes back aboard and rescues Little Prue, the Jenkins fourteen-year-old tomboy daughter. David Jenkins and Big Prue are killed.

Little Prue comes to live with the Underwoods and chooses Ashton as her guardian. Potts brings in

"Burning tanks of oil boiled over." from *Tract Number 3377*.

Chapter 14   119

wells for both Ashton and the Underwoods. Ashton uses some of his money to pay for an operation for his mother. She regains her senses and moves back into their house. Little Prue goes to live with her. Ashton becomes engaged to Anna, who goes off to Boston to study voice. There is an estrangement between Ashton and Anna, partially because Mrs. Walburg doesn't approve of Anna and shows it. Anna studies voice in Turin. A fire threatens Ashton's wells. Ashton rushes to his wells to fight off the fire. In doing so, he falls from a cliff and is severely injured. When he regains consciousness, he wants Anna. Een prevails upon Mrs. Walburg to send a wire to Anna. She does, writing, "Ashton and I need you, Forgive and come at once."(*TN 372)* Anna does, and a wedding is planned.

This is another melodramatic love story with the lovers being all too pure and good, but because of the more believable minor characters it's an interesting story. This is also one of the first books to deal with the changes that come about as a result of sudden wealth. Anna was already getting a better education than her parents before oil was struck. But she was able to get a piano and study music in Boston because of the new wealth. Her parents bought and furnished a new home; otherwise, they seem little changed. Little Prue became much more sophisticated because of her better schooling. But there is no example of crude, nouveau riche behavior, such as in *The Spotter*, and no feeling of superiority as exhibited by Mr. Smedley in *Oil Well in the Woods*.

Chapter 15

Oil and a Church in West Virginia

The next oil novel also deals with changes, but not personal changes. Instead, it concerns the changes that occur in a town as a result of the boom and the new wealth. In *The Church On Quintuple Mountain: A Story of Pennsylvania Oil Country Life Possibly a Trifle Exaggerated in Spots* (1912) by Bion Butler[*], one of the local gamblers decides that the town needs a church. As the title suggests, this is a light-hearted little book full of nice people. It's a never-never land, but it's fun. The gambler discusses with his customers why he thinks the town needs a church:

> "They's another small matter we want to speak about while they's silence in the house and we have the time. The Sand Pump this morning tells about the sermon juggler that has been doing a few turns over in the Citizens' Exchange building, and he says this town is overdone with gin mills and gambling hells and disreputable theaters, and it is a scandal in the sight of the Almighty that it hasn't got a church."
>
> "Let's go down and put a sixty-quart shot under him and pass him up to Happy land, "suggested Walden.
>
> The proposition found some favor, but Watson held up his hand for attention, and proceeded:

---
[*]Bion Butler is the author of a history of a Moore County North Carolina Presbyterian church, Old Bethesda at the Head of Rockfish (1933).

Cover image from *The Church on Quintuple Mountain*

"Listen, gentlemen. Some of you may feel owly at a statement like this, but when you come out of your spasm, we are all backing the parson in Quintuple. Ain't any of you so old but you remember when Jonah come to Nineveh that town had to call off the graft and overhaul the police force. It's always that way. Quintuple is no jay town. We have an all-right faro layout, and schools that are at the head of the class, and people that starts out early in the day, and the best oil sand the drill ever tapped, bar none, and stores, and hotels, and a saloon that is talked about clear to New York, and all that kind of public conveniences, and we overlooked one of the best bets. How can you recommend your town to people anywhere else unless you can say you have a church?" (CQM 4-5)

So Watson raises the money, and the folks of the town build the Church, but the Rev. Mr. Clark is not willing to take it at first because of the source of the money used to build it. After some arguments he accepts it. Then he asks whether they are his denomination or not. They say they don't care: "You can have her Episcopal, Calvinist, Hellgalerian, or even Jew if you want, ..." (CQM 34) He says he is Methodist, and everyone agrees that it will be a Methodist church.

When the church opens, the narrator uses this opportunity to express his opinion about democracy in the town:

> A gratifying congregation filled the church on the succeeding Sunday morning, and filled the pavement in front and the vacant lot at the side as well. Oil operator, business man, driller, men from

the leases, around the town, Watson the gambler in a prominent pew near the altar, Perkins the saloon keeper, Thompson the president of the Oil Exchange, listening to the Poetry of the scripture lesson instead of the clamor of the bull ring, women and little people, a cosmopolitan representation of a democratic community, crowded the house and overflowed it in all directions outside.

No better exhibition of absolute democracy ever existed than at Quintuple. The driller of today might be the well owner of tomorrow. Equality found as much of a footing in the oil country as is possible in Christendom. The pastor looked down from the pulpit on a flock that any man of God might envy him.

The ushers had no difficulty in placing the worshippers. The tool dresser who had no pew was seated beside the banker who had one, and nobody ever thought to question it. *(CQM 39)*

One of the pleasures of reading this book is the frequent use of gambling and oil metaphors. In referring to the pastor, Watson says: "He has a backbone like a joint of six-inch casing. *(CQM 38)* Another time he says of him: "The parson is a good man, third sand, full head and fine gas pressure, and bound to pay out the money we have tied up in the venture." *(CQM 145)* Watson's daughter is in love with David Logan, a local oil man. She tells him that he is rarely enthusiastic, and he responds, "Well, may be I do keep my finger on the pressure gauge, but that does not signify but what the full head of steam is there." *(CQM 118)*

Much of the plot of the book is about the gradual

reforms Rev. Clark makes in the town. He gets the gambler and saloon keepers to close down. There are of course two love relationships to be sorted out. And there are some stories involving the oil business. One particularly interesting tale involves Dave's success in finding oil while looking for gas. Willock makes him a good deal:

> "You get the lease and we will pay for it. In addition, for your work we will give you the oil right if you want it, and we take the gas right. We will pay you for drilling as many wells as we want put down. If they have gas, they are our wells. If you have the fool luck to find oil and no gas, they are your wells and no cost to you."
>
> "That looks cheaper than stealing for me. Just make a little note of it on paper, so we can see what it sounds like when you read it over again, but make it say that I get the oil and you get the gas in case we find both in one well. Or, does that sound to you too much like the white man's way of dividing with the Indian he had been hunting with when the white man said he would take the turkey and give the Indian the buzzard, or give the Indian the buzzard and keep the turkey himself?"
>
> "That's the way it shows up, Dave. But as long as it's buzzard we're after and the buzzard looks good, why we take the buzzard as fast as you can get it to us. If there was any oil on the lot, it would be different, but as there is about as much chance of finding oil up on the Grimesby as there is of finding drillers in heaven, I am willing to let you have the turkey for getting us the buzzard. We'll be mighty glad to have you get it on these terms." (CQM 92-3)

Dave of course finds oil and no gas. The "octopus," Standard Oil, shows up and offers him $400,000 for his holdings. He bargains with them and ends up with $500,000. The narrator comments on all this: "These things show the potentialities of the oil country and in a measure explain why Quintuple traveled so indifferently at such a rapid gait. It makes clear why money had so little value and why David Logan could treat so nonchalantly with the man who offered him such riches. Money was far too common to worship as is done everywhere else." *(CQM 99-100)* The nonchalance spoken of here by the people of Quintuple is exhibited by the author of the book, and it is one of the more entertaining of the early oil novels.

Chapter 16

Gauging and Scouting

The last of the early novels about the Pennsylvania oilfield, published in 1916, was a book for older boys, *"646" and the Trouble Man* by Charles H. Oliver. All I have been able to discover about Oliver is that he had worked for Standard Oil for thirty years. I learned this from a New York *Times* article also published in 1916.

In this novel, Oliver treats one area not covered in earlier oilfield fiction, gauging, and the importance of the telegraph to this operation. Also important to the novel is scouting and its connection to selling futures.

The novel begins with its hero, Jack Somers, in college, accepted by his classmates and a baseball star. In an overly written first scene, Jack tells his classmates that he must leave college and go to work. His mother has written to him about his father having a stroke and then other troubles:

> Then, you know, Jack, they say trouble never comes singly—the old 'Yack Yam' has gone to water. That was the old stand-by. The old Blaney farm lease, that has been in litigation for years, was decided against your father, and he will be compelled to pay back all the money he received from the oil he sold. This is a great injustice, as that lease belonged to your father; but they got some people to do some false swearing, and you know if father could not win

it fairly he would not have it at all *("646" 99-100)*

Jack explains that he has been offered a job with his father's former partner, Mr. Morrow. He has his choice of working in the office with Morrow or working in the field for one of Morrow's friends. Jack explains his choice:

> I'm choosing the field work. I like the country, I like the work. I love the smell of the crude oil as it comes green and frothy from the ground. I like to watch the cable as it comes hundreds of feet out of the earth, dripping the oil on the derrick floor and spraying it for yards around over the trees and bushes and around the derrick. I like the oil country people, the driller, the tool dresser, and the roustabout. Most of them are large of heart as well as large of frame, and as brave as they are big. "I have seen them go into a burning derrick after a comrade, when by some accident the gas had got on fire and exploded; have seen them go back into a hell of fire and drag him out, then fall, black and scorched, just outside of the fire line. Anyone in need or in trouble of any kind is always helped, and God pity the man who stands back and refuses to help. He will not last long in that country. *("646" 99-100)*

He goes on to tell about his father's and Mr. Morrow's great well and its discovery:

> "I don't suppose any of you fellows ever saw an oil well drilled in. What I mean is, when the drill reaches the sand. That is the important moment for the oil operator. When Mr. Morrow wired father that the 'Yack Yam' expected to reach the pay the

following day, father and I went to Parker's Landing and drove out to the Campbell farm where the well was located. We arrived about four o'clock, in the afternoon. Billy Steele, the driller, was hard at work turning the temper screw. One could see by the vibration of the cable in the hole that the jars were hitting at every stroke of the walking beam. Mr. Morrow was in the derrick, seated on the bellows, looking very sober — in fact, every one around the rig looked serious. Very often the driller and the tool dresser on a well take as much interest in getting a good well as any of the owners.

"When we went in Mr. Morrow looked up and said, 'Well, Somers, it doesn't look very good. We are deep enough now, and should have the pay, but instead we are drilling on something that is as hard as flint. If it doesn't soften up pretty soon I won't give much for her. This is practically a wildcat, and we are farther south than any of them, but we are in a direct line with a lot of good wells, and I think it should extend this far, at least.'

"Turning to the driller, he asked, 'Billy, how is she cutting now?'

"Billy answered, 'Hard as hell; not cuttin' at all; just wearin' away.'

"At six o'clock we went up to the boarding house for supper, both Mr. Morrow and father feeling pretty blue. Afterwards we went back to the well. Mr. Morrow asked Billy if there had been any change, but Billy just shook his head and kept on turning the cable. We all sat around, quietly waiting. If this well should prove to be a dry hole I knew it would be a hard blow to Mr. Morrow and father, as both had their last dollar in it, and some borrowed money besides. All at once Billy jumped up on the derrick stool and commenced to let out screw. Then he jumped down and put his ear close to the hole and sprang up again, yelling, 'For God's sake, grab those derrick lamps and run! I think we have her!'

"Mr. Morrow grabbed one of the derrick lamps, handed it to me, and took the other himself, and cried, 'Run for your life!' Father and the tool dresser had started for the boiler; and were trying to drown out the fire. Mr. Morrow and I hadn't got more than a hundred feet from the derrick when the oil came out of the hole with a rush, and the 'Yak Yam' was an oil producer! They connected the lead lines to the casing head, and in a short time had the oil going into the oil tanks. *("646" 99-100)*

Jack continues with his long monologue to his friends by telling his friends about the boom town of Parker's Landing:

Mr. Morrow, father, and I drove back to Parker's Landing, at that time the wild and woolly oil town of the world. It was lighted up with huge gas lamps all along River Avenue, which fronted on the Allegheny River. Every other house along the avenue was a hotel or boarding house, every hotel or boarding house had a bar, and every bar was a gambling joint of some kind, running wide open.

Down at the landing was a large steamboat, owned and run by the famous Ben Hogan. On this boat he ran a big bar and dance hall. Everything was furnished up in grand style. A fine brass band from Pittsburgh played all night, or until everyone was tired out or too drunk to dance any longer.

At one time this little city made the oil market for the world. Oil was the talk of the town. The streets were crowded with drillers, producers and tool dressers, pipe-line men and roustabouts, all wearing high-topped boots, blue shirts, and broad-brimmed hats, many of them sprinkled with sand pumpings. The smell of oil was in the air, as the fluid came from some well or tank up the river and floated down past the town. The road along River Avenue was hub deep with mud, and one could often see six and eight horses hauling a load that two could pull on good roads. This is life in a new oil town. *("646" 12-3)*

Earlier, Jack had told his friends about how a well was connected to a pipeline.

When you get an oil well down, it flows oil out, if there is enough gas in the hole force it up; if not, they put tubing and sucker rods in and pump it out. The oil goes into a tank at the well; this tank is connected to the pipe line and the oil runs by gravity, or is pumped from the wells to the large receiving tank of the pipe-line company. The man who accepts the oil from the producers, and runs it into the pipe line's tank at the station, is called a gauger. *("646" 7)*

He then told them about his father being an engineer and what he did:

The men on the station are called engineers; they pump the oil from local station to one of the main-line stations; that is, one of the stations that pump oil from the oil country to refineries at Cleveland, Philadelphia, and other points. Every engineer must be a telegraph operator, as the pipe-line company has its private wires all over the oil country, so that in case anything happens to the lines quick notice may be given to the pumping end and the pump shut down. *("646" 7-8)*

Jack explains that as a child he spent lots of time at the station and became an expert at sending and receiving telegraph messages. Now Jack tells Mr. Morrow that he wants to learn all of the jobs in the field, to "go into the connection gang — help to lay the lines, build the stations, construct the telegraph lines, and learn all the tricks." Mr. Morrow says that he is pleased. He knows that Jack will find the pipe line tough at first but that he will harden to it. Morrow says, " I would consider you a first-class engineer, as you understand a boiler, a pump, and an engine as well as the best of them." *("646" 22)*

He says that he thinks Jack only needs experience in the construction of a pipeline in order to hold down any position in a pipe line company. He also tells Jack that the company of Mr. Galman, Jack's new boss, is building a new six-inch line from the Hilliard Mills in the oilfield to Cleveland — more than a hundred miles — and that they will be constructing four large pumping stations and a telegraph line. Morrow says that Galman is a very strict man but a very fair one.

Galman wires Morrow that Jack can start the next day but that he will not be making "any fancy salary," and he will have to take pot luck — he will receive no special favors.

When Jack stops off at his home, he notices the

beauty of the area. He sees nothing wrong with oil running out onto the ground:

> The Somers home stood in what was called "The Bluff." From it was obtained a view for miles up and down the Allegheny River. When part way up the bluff, Jack stopped to rest and to gaze into the beautiful valley. It had never looked so good to him before. From where he stood he saw the grand old hills far and near. The leaves had their first tinge of color, as it was the fall of the year.
>
> Just above the bridge was Fox Island, where were located three or four oil wells, almost concealed from view by large oak and chestnut trees. They were cleaning out, or completing one of them through the sand, for very few minutes the oil would spurt far above the top of the derrick, then settle back over the trees and bushes, and as the sun caught the falling spray all the colors of the rainbow were visible. Just above was an island where the Clarion River emptied into the Allegheny. About a mile farther up was the little village of Foxburg. Far down the river Jack saw the black smoke of a locomotive, winding along the river's edge. A minute more, and he saw the engine poking its nose around the Cat-Fish bend, drawing a string of empty oil cars on their way to Oil City. Then it disappeared, to reappear just below the Rattlesnake Falls. On the high bank, directly across the river, he saw the row of iron tanks, all filled with crude oil. Halfway down the bank to the river was all that remained of old Number 51, that had been struck by lightning and set on fire.("646" 25-6)

Then he remembers the horror of the fire caused by the lightning:

> How well he remembered that night! Though it was long after midnight, no one thought of going to bed, for all the old timers knew that after it had burned for a certain length of time the tank would cave in and the oil boil over. "Then there'll be hell," was murmured. The pipe-line people calculated they might expect the first overflow at about two o'clock. Shortly after that time the tank collapsed with a crash, sending the burning oil down to the river. In a few minutes it had spread from bank to bank, and soon the river was a stream of flame, "from which sputtering tongues leaped and danced. As the swiftly running current bore the burning oil down the stream, what a scramble there had been to reach the high ground of the bluff! Quite a number of the slower ones had blistered backs before clearing the fire zone. In a short time after the burning oil struck the river, most of the long rows of stores and business houses that stood on the flat, and made River Avenue, were a roaring mass of twisted flames. *("646" 26-7)*

After visiting his family and telling them about his new job, Jack heads to Hilliard by rail and gives an interesting picture of the narrow gauge railroads of the area:

> The railroad and rolling stock of this system were among the first things in their lines. The locomotive and three cars were small, toy-like, and unsightly. Ten miles an hour was the scheduled speed of the little train, as it rattled and wobbled along two crooked and rusted streaks of iron that had been carelessly strung through the wild and hilly country.

Up and down, and to both sides, the rails wandered in their course. The small streams encountered were followed along their winding ways to headwaters, and then the roadway departed, commonly climbing one steep grade and descending another in quest of another stream that would provide grade and run in the general direction of the objective point, which was as much as the roadway itself did. When a rock, too large to be removed, reared itself in the path of the road finders, they had built the road around it, for curves were as common to it as links to a chain.

Over this imperfect roadbed the diminutive train rolled, rooted, and lurched, every twist accentuating the constant creaking of the car timbers. Travel was uncertain, and delays were common, but the travelers made allowances, and no one worried about schedules, for the train had the right of way — there was but one a day. *("646"31-2*

On the train, he met other workers heading to the pipeline job, some experienced, some "greenhorns." The men were given thirty minutes to eat before starting work. Men shared their grub with those who had none. His crew of 150 men were divided into three crews: the tong, or construction gang of forty men, the telegraph crew of ten, and the ditching gang of one hundred. There were thirty teams of draft animals to haul and string the pipe. They made great progress the first day and the narrator tells us more about the setup of a pipeline camp:

At three o'clock in the afternoon the vanguard arrived at Hilliard's, a town of about a dozen houses, two stores, and a blacksmith shop. The hamlet was the terminal of the Shenango Railroad that operated between Shenango and Hilliard's. It was the receiving point for miles. Piles of six-inch pipe, thousands of telegraph poles, and coils of wire were stacked along the sidings, as well as other material used in pipe-line construction. On a string of flat cars were two huge Worthington pumps, a battery of four stationary boilers, and pipe fittings by the thousands. In a box car were barrels of sugar, coffee and tea by the box, jam and dried meats of all kinds, beans and canned fruits by the barrel — all for the commissary department.*("646"34)*

The tong gang and the dining crew lived in four tents. The dining and sleeping tents were 16' by 30'. The crews ate on two long tables and slept in cots in two rows. The camp was moved once a week, and in that time the crew could lay about sixty miles of pipe. Previously the path for the line had been surveyed, right-of-way purchased, and the land cleared. So when the construction crew arrived everything was ready for placing the joints.

Jack's crew started work at seven, beginning with the rustlers moving ahead to remove the rings protecting the threads. Jack had laid two-inch pipe but with the six-inch sometimes his tongs would slip, and it would jar his whole body. By afternoon, his crew has laid one hundred and twenty five joints. Jack didn't like his foreman, Red Murray, a huge man weighing over 250 pounds. He acted friendly when Galman was around, but when Gallman wasn't, he cursed the men, threatened them, and intimidated them.

The work went well and within two weeks, the men had completed over eight miles of pipe line. Then Jack made an enemy of Red:

On a Saturday, Galman was personally in charge of the work. A creek crossing with a very steep bank on each side had been reached, and required a very difficult "down bend." When they came to a bend of any size the men had to stop and build a fire to heat the pipe, that it might be shaped. In this way much time was lost, as the gang was idle while the pipe was being heated. While some of the men were building the fire and getting ready for the bend, Jack suggested to Galman that they might span the stream with the pipe, place men with their tongs on it in an upright position, and enough of them, he thought, would give sufficient weight to bend the pipe as required.

"Red," who was standing near Galman, gave a hoarse laugh, almost an imitation of the braying of a donkey, and said something about a "sappy green-horn learning them how to lay a line."

Galman studied Jack intently for a minute, then, turning to the foreman, ordered, "Screw on a few joints, and we'll try it. The worst we can do is to break off one of the threads."

They did as Jack directed, and in a few minutes the "down bend" was completed, and as effectively as by the heating process, which would have required an hour.

Turning to Jack, Galman said, "Good for you, young man! The pipe-line people are looking for young men to-day who use their thinking caps."

There was a cruel glint in the foreman's eyes

when this compliment was passed, and Jack detected it.

"I'll not get any bouquets from that redfaced bully," he thought aloud. *("646" 37-8)*

Red makes it tough on Jack as he can, but Jack pays little attention until Red strikes one of his friends, a young sickly telegraph operator. Jack challenges Red and the fight is on:

"Now, sonny, back up a little," he said tauntingly. "Maybe a first-class slap would do you' as much good as the operator."

Now all the men liked the quiet, goodnatured boy, but that he would attempt to fight the bully was beyond their conception.

Jack walked up close to Murray and asked, "Are you ready?" "I'm always ready for a scrap," was the retort, but the words had scarcely passed his lips when Jack sprang forward, and with his open hand struck him across the face just as Red had struck the young operator. It was a stinging blow, and brought the blood.

Instantly the fight was on. It was great strength without control against great strength with perfect control — bewilderment against positive mental precision. Murray, stinging and smarting, body and mind, from the slap, rushed upon his smaller antagonist, but was met by hard fists driven by hard, fast muscles, directed by a quick-thinking mind, that landed every blow on the flabby face of the bully. *("646" 42)*

Jack chooses to punish Red rather than finish him

off quickly. He finally "brought oblivion" to Red. Galman has observed it all and even though he doesn't approve of scrapping admits that Red had it coming. Galman tells Jack that he is reassigning him to work on building "the largest oil-pump station in the world."

The narrator summarizes the work on the pump station:

> Within four months Mr. Galman and Jack Somers built the first pump station. From the blueprints prepared by the chief engineer they made the cement foundations, set the large rods that held the pump in place, and set the four large boilers. They raised the four immense smoke stacks, connected the pumps and boiler, and last of all connected the suction lines from the two large iron tanks to the pumps. *("646" 47)*

Mr. Morrow then tells Jack that Mr. Day has transferred him to Tiona as an engineer at a pump station. He will be working under the supervisor at Warren, Mr. Moss.

When Jack reports to work, he dislikes Mr. Moss immediately but seemed pleased with the job at Tiona:

> ... Moss went with him to Clarendon, a small town about ten miles from Warren. Here they were joined by the field foreman, Mr. Norris, a dark-skinned man with black mustache and small chin beard, who might have been taken for a Spaniard. Moss introduced Jack to Norris, and the three men started down the street toward Tiona, which was lo-

cated about a mile and a half below Clarendon. They came to a small local pipe-line station, equipped with a suction pump and boiler. Moss explained to Jack the station was used to pull the oil from the field wells, as the land lay very low and the oil would not gravitate from the wells. The suction pump would draw the oil and discharge it to the large station tanks at Clarendon. Jack was told he would be required to run this station for the gaugers and do the telegraphing, get the O. K. from the oil from the large stations, and blow the steam whistle to let the gaugers know their oil was en route. ("646" 61)

The narrator tells us that Mr. Norris had someone else picked out for the job, so he plans to see to it that Jack will quit. Jack has no trouble with the job the first day, but he discovers that he must telegraph in fifty runs because no oil had been run the previous few days because of high water. Jack meets the challenge by demonstrating his extraordinary ability to send telegraph messages.

Soon after arriving in Tiona, Jack meets, rescues, and becomes friends with a really odd young man, Fighting Gib. Gib works part time as a tool dresser and is known for his daredevil climbing of oil rigs. Jack sees him place his hand on the pulley block at the top of the rig and stand on his head. Then still on top, he dances a jig. He also claims that he can whip any man between Warren and Kane. Jack goes up to the rig to observe him more closely:

> He went on to the derrick floor; they were about ready to pull the tools out of the hole. The driller, a small man, was standing at the throttle. Fighting

Gib was ready to throw the bull rope on the wheel. He was over six feet tall, and built solidly from the ground up. He smiled as Jack stepped up on the derrick floor.

"He doesn't look like a quarrelsome man; I really like his face. He looks pretty good natured," Jack thought. As he came up the driller was saying to Gib, "I'll have to go into the engine house to reverse that engine. This thing is out of kilter. Throw on your rope, then watch the slack in the cable. That new rope doesn't work very well yet."

As the driller came around the "headache post," Jack stepped toward the brake, out of his way. The driller went into the engine house and after calling back to Gib, "Are you ready?" started the engine.

Gib threw on the bull rope, and stepped back to straighten out the slack. A kink in the cable entangled his foot, and in the treacherous grip of the rope he was dragged halfway round the shaft!

Jack sprang forward, caught the brake lever, and slammed it down so hard he fell with it. At the same time he yelled to the driller: "For God's sake, reverse your engine !"

From the engine house the driller saw Jack lying on the floor of the derrick, holding down the brake, but the escaping steam was making so much noise he could not hear his words. Shutting off the steam, the driller ran toward the derrick. One glance was enough; he rushed back and reversed the engine, and Gib dropped to the floor. Jack and the driller carried him out on the walk, beside the belt house. *("646" 66-7)*

Gib is unharmed and becomes Jack's fast friend.

Shortly after, on the Fourth of July, Jack and Gib go into Warren, and in an extended scene Jack replaces an injured catcher in a baseball game and becomes an instant hero by handling the fast ball of Rube Waddell and delivering the winning hit in the last inning.

In December, Norris and Moss still want to replace Jack with their man and are disappointed that Jack is still on the job. They decide to send him to Wardwell, in the wilderness, where there is no good place to board and inferior equipment. They assume he will soon get sick of it and quit. Jack is supposed to gauge and run the station. Jack thinks he is getting a promotion.

Gib tells Jack that he doesn't think he will like it there because there are only shanties in which to stay and board. Gib decides to move to Wardwell with him. Jack is appalled by the equipment at the station:

> Jack found it the most desolate place he had ever visited. The boiler house was just large enough for the boiler and a small boiler feed. There was only one window, and on the sill of this was nailed a board, which served as a telegraph table. The boiler looked as if it had come from the junk yard; there was one water cock on it—the one in the middle, and when the water got below that gauge, its stage was an unknown quantity. The crown sheet had been "roasted" so much, it looked like a washboard. The boiler feed was a small Cameron pump that ran just the same when it was putting water in the boiler as when it was pumping air. Jack learned all these things the first day after getting up steam and asking for orders to start the pumping.

"I don't think I'm hurt, he said, feeling his feet and leg." from *"646" and the Trouble Man.*

The oil pump, a little better than the boiler, was an old Blake, and had seen better days. Norris had fixed up the station especially for Jack. As he remarked to himself: "If that don't make that young man sick of his job, I don't know what will."*("646" 96-7)*

The bark peeler's shanty were he found room and board was no better. He is bothered by the snorers, and when he finally goes to sleep, he is awakened by the drillers and tool dressers changing tour at midnight. He doesn't fall to sleep until almost morning, and when he wakes up, he finds an inch of snow on his blanket.

When Jack sees the house cat fall into the batter being prepared, the cook says, "Thet's two times you've feld in that 'ere batter; if you fall in agin, it won't be fit ter use."*("646" 100)*

So Jack and Gib find a slab shanty in the woods just above the pump station and begin to cook for themselves. But Jack still has to contend with the dangerous boiler, and he has to cross the river in an equally dangerous boat, "made of old planks and slabs, too heavy of its own weight and when coated with ice it floated with barely two inches above water."*("646" 102)* Jack also has to go into tank houses which are exceedingly dangerous to enter because sometimes they are filled with gas. Jack considers quitting, but it is a matter of principle to stick it out.

Mr. Morrow, in the area to visit his daughter, who is visiting her grandfather in Warren, decides to check on how Jack is doing. First, he talks to Moss and Norris, who lie to Morrow about him, saying that Jack has almost destroyed the fine boiler and pump that they had provided him.

Morrow doesn't believe them and decides to visit Jack. Morrow meets an Irish couple who praise Jack to the sky. Then he goes to Wardwell and sees for himself the junk that Jack has had to keep operating. He is amazed.

Then he approaches Jack with a proposal for a different kind of work. Morrow thinks there is oil near his father-in-law's property:

> "Well, I understand that some parties have secured quite a lease out there, and are to start a well at once. Now, as soon as they get started to drill I want you to watch that wildcat well. If they should get a big well it would break the market, as it will open a new field. Do you realize what that would mean to our firm? If that well should prove a gusher, and we could get the information twenty-four hours in advance of the rest of the talent, it would mean a fortune! Now, I don't know of anyone better fitted than you to do this work. You have been around oil wells almost all your life, and you ought to know where the drill is hammering. You know how to determine depth by the number of coils on the bullwheel shaft; so they could not fool you very much as to how far in they are—if you could get into the derrick.
>
> "I believe, if I were you, I would cut out from here the first of the month and go back to Tiona, where you have a good boarding house. That will be only six or eight miles from where I understand the well is located. It will be on Tract 646. I will pay you the same as you are getting here, and if you make

> good, and we make a killing, I'll share the profits with you; So you have nothing to lose, and a chance to make some money. Somehow, I have great faith in that as an oilfield. *("646" 113-4)*

The narrator doesn't say whether or not Jack accepts Morrow's proposition, but he soon runs afoul of Moss and Parker:

> A few days later, about four o'clock in the afternoon, he received a message from Moss to run a tank of oil for a Mr. Rose. Jack had been informed that Moss and Norris were interested in this well, but it was known as the Rose well as it would not do to have their names appear in the lease. The tank was only a short distance from the station. Jack took his gauge pole, wrench, and thief tube, and started. He found the tank standing out exposed to the weather—no tank house, and no top on the tank. It had been snowing for a couple of days, and there were six inches of ice and snow on top of the oil. Owing to the frozen condition, it was with difficulty that he forced the gauge pole to the bottom of the tank.
> "Well, I wouldn't call that merchantable oil, and I don't think I'll run it." With this declaration he returned to the station, and sent Moss a message. The oil had not been steamed, he informed Moss, and was not in condition to run; he refused to run it. *("646" 116)*

Moss sends him a message to run the oil any way. Jack replies that the oil is not in condition to run, that it is unsteamed. Moss replies that he should run the oil as ordered. Jack still asserts that the oil was not in shape to run. Moss telegraphs back that he must run the oil or Moss would put someone on the job who would.

Gib asks Jack what he will do. Jack says he might be able to run it into the tank at their station but can't because the tank has three broken hoops. He tells Gib the oil has ice in it and is like liver. He doesn't think he can get enough steam in the boiler to push it through. Jack says he knows that it is a mistake but will do as ordered. Jack tells Gib to watch the boiler while he turns on the tank. Gib says he will, "I think it'll need watchin'; some of these days it will git up and git out of here!"

After a while, the station pump takes hold and the oil runs well at first because there is good oil in the line, but as the heavy oil comes in, the pump begins to slow up and soon it is barely moving even with 80 pounds of steam in the boiler. Jack turns a little more gas on, and Gib says, "If you turn any more gas into that old kittle, I'm goin' ter git out of here, before I'm helped out!" ("646" 119)

The pump starts running faster and Jack concludes that the line is broken. In the pump house, he finds that the gasket in the flange on the discharge line has blown out. Gib helps him get the line apart, put in a new gasket, and put it together again. This is difficult because they have to work in the dark because of fthe danger of fire from the oil and gas.

Once they finished the repair, they try again:

> After opening the stops on the suction and discharge, Jack turned steam into the pump. The piston rod worked back and forth a few times, then

stopped. Jack ran the steam up to ninety pounds, but the pump would not move. Gib commented: "Every pound you put on her is jist increasin' your chances fer to be lifted out of here in a hell of a hurry!" Jack stepped around in front of the boiler, turned out the gas, and replied:

"Well, old man this settles it. That line is plugged from here to Warren, and I am through at Wardwell." *("646" 119-20)*

Jack then sends a message to Moss explaining what he has done and what the result is. He finishes by resigning effective immediately.

When Moss finds out what happened, he knows he is in trouble, so he gets all the messages from the telegraph operator and hides them.

Moss and Norris decide to put the blame for the stuck lines on Jack. But first they must find out whether Jack has copies of the messages. They try to be nice to him until they get the messages. When they think they have them, Moss tells Jack he is fired. Jack tells him to look closely at the messages. They are carbon copies. Jack has the originals in his pocket. Norris and Moss try to take them from him, but Jack easily beats the two of them even when Moss attacks him with a piece of pipe. When Moss recovers, he threatens Jack with the law, but Gib and two drillers have witnessed the skirmish.

As Gib and Jack leave for Tiona, they take one final trip across the river and then shove the dangerous boat into the water and let it drift away.

Jack sends the messages to Morrow with an explanation of what happened and soon Moss and Norris are fired.

Jack begins his work as a scout for Morrow. In the first three weeks there, he visits the tract where the well is to be drilled. The first time he is there, he finds the rig timbers on the ground. He realizes that in this new territory a gusher would cause havoc in the oil market.

On the third trip out, Gib, who knows the country well, guides Jack. When Jack says that he needs a telegraph line to send messages to Morrow, Gib tells him about an old, abandoned line. Gib and Jack get new wire and start repairing the line.

As he is doing this work, he meets and rescues a beautiful young lady. He doesn't know she is Morrow's daughter, Wilma. Nor does she know that Jack is the son of her father's former partner.

Ben Miller, the son of Morrow's present partner, attempts to force himself on Morrow's daughter, but Jack defends her and easily beats Miller.

When Wilma writes Morrow about Ben Miller's attempt to attack her, Morrow tells Miller that Ben can't work for them any more. This leads to Miller leaving the firm and working with one of Morrow's rivals, Z. Z. Smith and Company an unsavory company: "Their object was to make money—honestly, if convenient; dishonestly, if necessary." Miller sets out with them to get Morrow:

> The firm of Morrow & Miller had been speculative in its dealings, the majority of which had terminated profitably, due to Morrow's foresight. At the time they dissolved partnership there was a difference of opinion on the market's tendency. Morrow favored "going short," but Miller was certain the

market would go higher, and it was a "good buy." He pointed out that the Bradford and New York fields were on the wane, and that there was nothing in sight to break the market. The Smith clique felt as Miller did. They had plenty of capital behind them, and were ready to buy anything in the way of oil that Morrow had to offer. They whispered it about that they would have "the old man's hide on the fence in less than sixty days."

"If we work this thing right," said the elder Smith, "we'll make one of the biggest killings this county ever heard of. We'll smash Morrow so flat he'll never get on his feet again!" ("646" 148)

Whether "646" makes an important well is important to Morrow's strategy, so Jack's getting information to him fast is important. Jack gets the line repaired and sets up a s code using odd numbers so that no one can intercept his messages to Morrow. Jack writes Morrow that the crew of "646" is ready to spud in. Then Jack and Gib complete the telegraph line to within a mile of the wildcat. Here they build a shanty.

Jack visits the well again, and the driller tells him they have drilled to about 800 feet, but Jack can tell from the amount of cable that they are at 1200 feet. Gib makes another trip to the well and reports they are at 1800 feet and he thinks they are at the top of the sand. Then their ability to check is closed off:

> The next morning, when Jack arrived within sight of the well, he found everything boarded up and six men guarding the well, each armed with a shotgun. He was halted more than a thousand feet

from the well, and told to "back track," as the guard called it. The man explained to him no one was allowed to approach the well except the owners and drilling crew. The drillers and tool dressers were in there now, and would not be permitted to come out. Their meals would be carried to them and places fixed for them to sleep. *("646" 161)*

Jack makes plans to sneak by the guard. He has Gib get him a black rubber coat, a hat, and a pair of boots. Scouting was dangerous work as other scouts discovered:

> By noon there were half a dozen men, mostly scouts, on the grounds, but they got no further than the guards. Two of the scouts tried to steal past the guards, but were discovered. A charge of shot went singing over their heads, too close for comfort, and they beat a hasty retreat. "The other barrel would not have gone over your heads, but into your hides," the guard told them. "Our orders are to hit, not to scare, and if you try that ag'in, that is what you'll git. This is private property, and you have no business here." *("646" 162)*

The first night, when Jack sneaked in, he could tell from the conversation that the well had not been completed. The narrator explains how important the information was that Jack was trying to get:

> The Fourth Avenue brokers, Smith & Company, were keeping close watch, by field men, on "646," as were several other brokers and large oil companies. When the Smith people heard that "646" was expected to reach the sand in a few days they sent

one of their most expert field men to watch the well, and in addition detailed Ben Miller, at the elder Miller's suggestion, to scout duty. Smith & Company and Miller had no faith in the well as an oil producer, but, as the elder Smith analyzed the situation, it was always best to be on the safe side. It was a foregone conclusion that if "646" proved a dry hole the market would go up, possibly over a dollar a barrel. The market hovered at about eighty cents a barrel for crude oil, and positive information on the well would place the recipient in a position to make great sums of money, provided his information preceded that of all others — it was a matter of time, and then quick action. This resulted in Smith & Company maintaining two men in the vicinity of the well, to have the most advanced information rushed to them the minute anything happened. It was a case of suspense while the drill neared the telltale stroke; a mystery was made of "646," which had been boarded up to baffle every attempt of scouts and newspaper men, oil producers, and oil men who had gathered in the vicinity of the well to secure an inkling as to what was going on inside. Attempts were made to bribe the guards, but they were futile, and no information leaked out. *("646" 165-6)*

Jack makes two more visits to the well but learns little. Many of the scouts believe that the well is dry but that the owners are keeping up the appearance of drilling in order to dispose of their lease holdings.

Ben Miller has grown weary of the woods and is gathering second-hand information from a barroom in Warren. Jack is puzzled and discouraged when on the fourth night of the mystery, he makes a discovery:

As he approached the rig, Jack could hear the creaking of the walking beam, and before he reached the derrick the smell of fresh oil came to his nostrils. He knew what that meant—they had struck the pay. In a moment he was under the derrick. There he could smell the oil plainly. He crawled over to where they dumped the sand pumpings through the floor. Soon he had the pocket of his rubber coat full of sand. He heard the men above him talking.

"We have only gone through the shell, and she has filled up almost a thousand feet. There is quite a bunch of gas, and I'm afraid she will drill herself in."

Jack could not understand why the beam was running right along, for he could not hear anything inside the casing. He afterward discovered they had taken the block out of the pitman, and, to anyone at a distance, the beam had that jerky motion common to a beam when drilling. The temper screw was not attached to the cable, and it was this that was fooling the curious and anxious outside the lines. *("646" 167)*

Jack gets back to the shanty at four and tells Gib what he has discovered. They have to wait until seven to telegraph Morrow, but they will still be well ahead of anyone with the information.

Gib is sent to Warren with the oil sample to express mail it to Morrow. While there, he goes to the bar and recognizes Ben Miller from Jack's description. Gib decides to put one over on Ben. He tells the bartender that he has been working out on the "646" for several weeks, so he is really thirsty. Miller hears him and offers to buy him a drink. Miller then tries to pump him for information. Gib says he has been sworn to secrecy. Then he tells Miller, "Yes, you look like a purty nice kind of a feller, and I don't mind tellin' you, but keep your trap closed — we're through the sand, and have run two screws in the slate, and that hole is so durned dry we jist git dust every time we run the bailer." *("646" 173)* Miller rushes to send a coded telegraph message to his father that the well is dry.

So Ben's father and Smith have their game plan — they will take every barrel of oil that Morrow offers, for there is no other new source of oil available. They believe that oil will go up in price by ten to twenty cents a barrel.

Meanwhile, Morrow has taken $250,000 with him to the exchange at Oil City. The narrator describes the battle between the longs and shorts:

> All day long the Smith crowd led the market. They continued on the buying end, taking up oil in five- and ten-thousand barrel lots. Under their constant demands the price had advanced from seventy-seven to seventy-nine in fifty-thousand barrel blocks. Morrow as regularly unloaded, and as quickly as his opponents bid he delivered. Other brokers followed, and seventy-nine and one-eighth was bid for small lots. When the gong sounded for the day, Morrow was short over three hundred thousand barrels, most of it disposed at seventy-nine or seventy-nine and one-fourth. (176)

The next morning, Jack sends Morrow another cipher message that ""646" had made a nice flow but was under control. Then Morrow sells more and more:

Morrow instructed his floor men to sell all they could on the market. The divergent methods of the Smiths and Morrow were to the front immediately after the market opened The Smiths offered seventy-nine and one-fourth for two hundred and fifty thousand barrels. There was no response, and they offered seventy-nine and one-half. Morrow promptly supplied them at the increase.

"I think," said Miller, "we'll have Q. G. on the run soon."

"Well," said Smith, "this market ought to go to eighty-two or eighty-three today."

They were interrupted; one of Morrow's men offered five hundred thousand barrels at seventy-nine and one-half.

"We'll take that," called Smith. "Have you any more ?"

"Yes, five hundred thousand more at the same."
"That is ours also," answered Smith.

Then six scouts arrived in Tiona and telegraphed the exchange that "646" was an oil well of unknown size. Then word came that it was making one hundred barrels an hour and that the crew could not shut her in. The Smith's thought it was a flash in the pan and continued to buy and Morrow to sell short. Word came that the well was out of control with a steady flow of 100 barrels an hour. Then the market went to pieces:

The exchange became the scene of a panic as the men, wildly excited, fought to unload. Oil was offered at seventy-five, seventy-four, then seventy-three — nothing bid — seventy-two, seventy-one, seventy, sixty-nine, and when the gong sounded and hushed the turbulence, the market had dropped to sixty-four! In the brief session a change of fifteen and a half points had been made in the price, and Smith & Company were believed to have been wiped out. *("646" 179)*

Miller said that he had put every cent he had in the market and was a ruined man.

A few days later, Jack is able to secure leases on three hundred acres near the well from a man he had aided earlier.

In hopes of seeing Wilma again, Jack says that he will check the telegraph wire to be sure there is no trouble with it. When he meets her, he discovers that she too knows telegraphy and the oil business:

> Do you know, if I had known you were coming I would have hung out 73 on one of the poles."
> "Then you know what 73 stands for?" queried Jack.
> "Sure; a telegrapher's best regards."
> "And G.M.?"
> "Good morning."
> "O.T.?"
> "Off tour."
> "SE?"
> "Busy on another wire."
> "Oil?"
> "Wire — this more important."
> Jack looked at her in astonishment as she answered his questions without hesitation.
> "Are you from the oil country?"
> "To be sure; I am an oil-country girl. I'm from 'up the creek.'"
> "So am I." *("646" 183)*

The book ends happily as Jack and Wilma discover each other's identity and acknowledge their love. Jack and Gib are rewarded handsomely by Morrow for their work in scouting and obtaining the leases.

This books is at its best when the narrator reports what the author knows best—the oil business. It is overwritten and sentimental when treating social and familial issues. I know of no other novel which deals so explicitly with the details of building a pipe line, running a pump station, gauging, and scouting, particularly the importance of scouting to the business of the brokers on the exchange.

Historically, "646" was a very important well. The Jamestown Oil Company brought it in in Cherry Grove Township of Warren County, Pennsylvania in 1862. At the time, it was the the largest gusher in the world. Hundreds of wells were drilled in the surrounding area over the next few months. Within a year, the population of Cherry Grove Township may have reached 10,000. But production soon plummeted, and by 1863 the boom was over.

Chapter 17

Novels of the 1940s and 1950s

The novels discussed in previous chapters were written at or near the time of the events described. Most of the authors had first-hand experience in the oil regions. The authors of the 40s and 50s have had to rely on their reading to find information to put in their stories. These novels may be placed in the broad category of historical novels. Like the earlier novels, parts of the novels are well-written, others parts not so well done.

Out of the Sand, by E. George Lindstrom was published in 1940. Although it had been many years since the boom days of Pennsylvania oil, Lindstrom had some first hand experience with the later years of that boom having lived in Oil City. He was born in Sweden in 1879, but in 1881, his family moved to Oil City. He attended public school there. He started working in the composing room of the *Oil City Derrick* in 1901. In 1935, he published his *Oil Creek Tales*. (http://library.case.edu/digitalcase/datastreamListing.aspx?PID=ksl:ech-leg#0). His novel is set before and during the early years of the oil boom, so he has done extensive research. He provides a list of his sources:

> "Out of the Sand" is a new historical novel based on discovery of oil, and in order to make this story live on the screen, stage, radio, or between the covers of a book, it is necessary to sacrifice much detail

to action. The story and locale are based on history, but the characters have no reference to persons living or dead. Any similarity to cities or persons is coincidental except names listed at bottom of page. E. George Lindstrom is indebted for much of the research material to P. C. Boyle, Oil City Derrick; James B. Borland, Franklin News; E. T. Stevenson, Titusville Herald; Ida Tarbell, author "History of Standard Oil"; C. Birtceil, Pithole driller; J. J. McLaurin, A. Smiley, C. C. Leonard; Frank W. Bowen, Oil City Blizzard; Speer and Fitts families, pioneers; H. Gordon Johnson. Mrs. T. W. Spieth, Philadelphia, Pa.; Mrs. Sarah Wymer. (OOS 10)

Lindstrom's novel is melodramatic and sentimental. It begins before the first oil well with the protagonist, Johnny, a ten-year old, being mistreated by a drunken father. Each day, the father chains the boy when the father goes off to drink. His mother steals a key, makes a copy, and allows her son to move about while his father is gone. One day, the father, while away, is killed in a storm. Johnny's mother dies soon after, and Johnny leaves home and wanders about. He is taken in by a kind hermit, Tim Timlin. They live happily together until Tim becomes destitute, sick, and hungry. Johnny tries to steal a loaf of bread, but he is caught and taken away from Tim and placed by a concerned judge with a good farm family, James and Jennie Spears, who place him in a good school. There, he is bullied, but Mr. Spears hires Professor White to teach him how to fight. He learns well and soon conquers the chief bully, Grimes Lemle, afterwards his sworn enemy and major villain in the oilfield later.

There he also meets Katie Campbell and falls in love with her and remains so throughout his life.

Johnny sees firsthand the first big oil discovery in Titusville. He carries the message from Uncle Billy Smith, the driller, to Drake. He has oil fever and loves oil even more than he does Katie. She tells him that she will have nothing to do with him if he leaves the farm and goes chasing after quick and unstable wealth in the new oilfields. He chooses oil and, after many difficulties, is close to making a well. Lemle tries to sabotage it by dropping a six-foot pipe into the well: "'Let's see him drill through that!' he chuckled maliciously." (OOS 136-7) Shortly afterwards, there is a rush of gas that blows the pipe and tools high into the air. This is followed by a "gushing black column shooting hundreds of feet upward." (OOS 137)

But even after he becomes fabulously rich, he is unhappy without Katie and goes to Philadelphia and New York and squanders his wealth. This part of the novel is based on events in the life of John Steele[*], better known as Coal Oil Johnny. John Steele, also an orphan, had inherited his money from the McClintocks, who took him in as a child. Steele left his wife and child and blew an inheritance of several million dollars in one year. Johnny Spear soon spends all his money and his well goes dry. He owes creditors, so he goes home penniless. When he reaches home, he learns that the Spears have both just died. Jennie died by being burned to death by upsetting an oil can by

---

[*] There is a wonderful article about John Steele available on line from a 1906 article in the New York Times: http://query.nytimes.com/gst/abstract.html?res=9D03EFDE103EE733A25754C0A96 79C946797D6CF

the stove. This is the same way that Mrs. McClintock, Johnny Steele's mother died.

The Spears had leased their land and had left all of their revenue to Johnny, but only if he returned to the farm and worked it. Katie Campbell was to keep the money in trust until he does. Katie has meanwhile become engaged to Neale Langor, who is in the mercantile business with her father. Neale is secretly investing in failing oil schemes.

John refuses to take any of the money. He tells her that it was all her doing and that she can take the money and throw it in the creek. John leaves for six months, but David, his friend and former partner, discovers him working on an oil raft during a disaster caused by a freshet, a system of flooding the creek to get enough water to propel the rafts:

> In their eagerness to get the precious fluid off to the industrial centers as quickly as possible, the oil men had tried to rush the creek before it was high enough, and one of the rafts drove its nose into a hump of mire not yet covered by the water.
>
> Back of it, load upon load strained and shoved at each other, timbers groaning and then splitting apart, with a grinding noise. Some plunged full force into the crush and upended, smashing the barrels they bore like eggshells and spilling the oil into the waters of the creek that bore its name. (OOS 179)

David has an opportunity to rescue John:

> The former millionaire was now tugging and pulling at the snagged raft, and as David watched, the raft began to give. John's muscles strained.

Slowly, sideways, the raft edged ahead and suddenly broke loose. The mass of barrel-laden boats behind John shifted toward the liberated raft, ground slowly to the other side and started swinging like an athlete, building up the momentum to propel a weight across the field. John hopped nimbly from one raft to another, giving each raftsman an order. But as he neared the one that was closest to the bank of the creek a raft whirled away from under him, and, as he leaped for another, his foot merely struck its edge and he fell backward into the path of the one behind.

The water wasn't very deep. Without hesitation, David, who was only a few yards away, plunged into the creek. Had John come up under one of the rafts, drowning would have been inevitable. David reached out and grabbed a handful of hair as it came to the surface and pulled John out of the path of danger. He towed him towards shore, where, in trying to get him to his feet, David also slipped and fell. The two of them went down into the oily mud, John underneath. David roared with laughter as the rescued man sat up, spewing oil and muck from his mouth, sloshing it from his face, arms and hands.
(*OSS* 179-80)

David and John, happy to be together again, take the money David has salvaged from their earlier well and begin to drill again. Just as previously, they use the spring pole method of drilling, which is dependent on their strength to propel the bit.

Once again almost desperate, they hit oil, and once again John is unhappy, though rich: "He had everything but Katherine, and that fact made everything else unimportant." (OSS 188) John returns to his old wastrel ways, first in Pithole and then in Pittsburgh. David stays and takes care of the well. Once again Lemle tries to sabotage their well. This time David is there to try to stop him. Lemle hits David with an iron bar. Then he throws the bar away from him, but he hits a bucket with a little nitroglycerin, and it explodes starting a fire. Fearful of being caught, Lemle rushes out leaving David to burn to death.

Earlier, Lemle had approached Katherine's husband, Neale, about helping him damage the well. Neale wouldn't agree to help but did nothing to stop the attack. Now he feels guilty, tell all he knows, and commits suicide. John has returned from his foolish exile upon the death of his partner. Meanwhile, a flood is threatening their town. It has led to the emptying of several oil tanks. And soon John has to go from rescuing people from the flood to avoiding the flames from oil and benzene on the waters. He tries to rescue one last man but is unable to do so because of the approaching flames. In the last line of the novel, he tells Katherine, with whom he has been reconciled, that the man was Grimes Lemle.

There is a lot of the historical events of the early Pennsylvania oilfield in this novel, even having a brief appearance of John Wilkes Booth. But ultimately it is not a well-written or believable novel. John disappears for long periods, and David carries the action. The characters are pasteboard figures. It's a melodrama.

Still another melodramatic oil novel, one worth only a brief mention is. *Go Devil* (1947) by Margaret Eyssens. It chronicles the life of Rand Bole in the Bradford area of the Pennsylvania oilfield. It begins with Rand, a poor boy with an intelligent mother and a feckless father. Rand is enchanted by Petty Dwyer, the daughter of their rich neighbor. Knowing that oil has been discovered nearby, the neighbor shrewdly forces Rand's father to sell him the farmstead for debts owed him. Soon every one in the neighborhood is rich but the Boles. Rand's father is killed in an oil well fire, and his mother becomes insane. He manages to grow up with the assistance of Abby, his mother's friend.

Rand becomes extremely ambitious and has an opportunity to get rich if he can just get a little money to complete the deal. An Irish hotelkeeper's daughter, Molly Lennon, advances him the money, and after great hardship he strikes it rich. He marries her and builds an oil company with her name, Lennon Oil. But when Petty Dwyer shows up, he is unfaithful to his wife.

There is much here about the oil business, and it is the only novel I know of describing the building of the great pipeline from the Bradford field to Williamsport. Historically, it was built by Byron Benson, who formed the Tidewater Pipe Company, and it was completed in June 1879 in spite of the opposition of Standard Oil. (API 452-456) In the novel, Brad is the president of the Seaboard Pipeline Company which also builds it in opposition to Rockefeller and Standard. In spite of his successes in the oil business, Rand is not happy. Too late, he sees the error of his way and repudiates the spoiled Petty and asks Molly to forgive him and stay with him, but she leaves, and the novel ends with him rich and unhappy.

And oil doesn't make Kim Dawson happy either. Kim Dawson is the heroine of Amy Fox's novel of the same name. Published in 1950, it traces the growth and destruction of an oil-boom town, Pit Hole.

Kim and her husband are already unhappy in their marriage when they arrive in Pit Hole. Her husband, Lance, has been wounded in the Civil War while fighting for the South. They had met when she nursed him back to health from a serious head wound. They marry even though he is an aristocrat from the plantation, Still Meadow, in Virginia and she is from an humble hill background. While in battle, Lance had been penned in a trench with a dying yankee soldier who told him about the oil wealth of his home in Western Pennsylvania. So Lance and Kim arrive in Pit Hole in June 1865, just as the boom is reaching its peak. The rapid construction is described in detail:

> Three weeks ago, in May, they had laid out the streets: First, Second, and Holmden — running the length of the place. There was Pig Alley and Murphy's Way and half a dozen other short cuts across the flats.
> Builders were coming in waves from Titusville and Oil City and Franklin, from Pittsburgh and Cleveland, and were putting up buildings at an incredible rate of speed. Last week in one day they built a hotel, and at sundown painted its name against the flat, blunt face. The Astor House, they called it. The smaller contractors were building houses for the people against the hillsides. One day a shower of old brown tents and pieces of tarpaulin would squat together like a growth of mushrooms;

the next, a row of houses. A bank and another on the way were on First Street now. A telegraph office, a newspaper, and unending hotel talk. (KD 47-8)

Kim, brought up by a hard-shell Baptist grandmother, immediately calls the place Sodom.

This is the only Pennsylvania oilfield novel that describes the important work of the teamsters, for Lance decides he will begin his work by using his team of mules to haul barrels of oil to the nearest market. Tim Foley, a new acquaintance, advises him not to use his team because they do not have the strength for the task. Lance insists that he will do it, and Foley says he should begin by carrying only three barrels. Lance goes to work for J. Greathouse, a man he immediately dislikes. Lance has already had a fight with one of the leaders of the teamster group, Cash Wilson. And Lance is soon attacked by him again:

> It happened so quickly that afterward there were a dozen versions of the affair. Cash Wilson did not answer Lance's threat but ran to his team and, gathering up the reins in one hand, cracked the whip with the other. The team plunged forward wildly, and the Conestoga wheels churned mud into a wave higher than a man's head, sideswiping the lighter wagon as they went by and crushing its wheels as if they were cardboard. One of the mules let out a shrill, unearthly squeal, and then the oil barrels began tumbling — one off the back of the wagon, one off the broken side. But the other, the top one, rolled forward; forward and came to rest, then rolled again. Both mules were down now, and the one that squealed had his hindquarters pinned under the weight of the barrel.

> Oaths were pouring in a sobbing breath from Lance's lips. He ran around the wagon and bent over the barrel, but his strength was gone from his hands. It did not even sway under his puny lifting. Others came now and, pushing him away, helped.
> (KD 86)

Lance is resilient. He soon has borrowed money for a new team, has loaded, and made the trip to Miller Farm. Then he gets to enjoy his new job:

> Lance unloaded the ten barrels he had hauled, got his tickets signed, and loaded up with empties. When the line hit the road they took it at a fast trot, the empties falling like hail on the wooden wagon beds. Up ahead someone began to sing. It was a rollicking, gay song that Lance had never heard before, and it concerned a gal named Susanna who was crying, and a roustabout with a banjo on his knee. The lilt of the song stirred him, and after a time he began to mutter a little under his breath. The Dawsons had always sung: in the big old parlors, on the hunt, as they walked the dusky path under oleanders and magnolias and misty gray oaks, with a pretty girl to listen and admire. This song was made for a rich, lilting baritone—it was made for Lance.
> "Oh! Susanna, do not cry for me,
> I come from Alabama 'wid my banjo on my knee."
> He swung into it with gusto and never knew when his mutter turned to a bellow.
> Maybe it was the song that filled him with exhilaration. Or maybe it was the trip itself—the feel

> of being a part of this great and unbelievable thing. It had been a good trip. It did a man good to feel the rumble of his own wagon beneath him and see the proud stepping of a pair of black queens such as he had. He laughed a little under his breath, feeling as if he had a good bourbon under his belt. *(KD 90-1)*

But he soon is too much into his enjoyments. He takes up with Fushia, a fancy girl from Mulroy's place. He leaves Kim stranded at home. As the title suggest, after the first part of the novel which features Lance, this is Kim's story. She refuses to leave her husband and endures his infidelity and foul temper. She adjusts to living this way while fending off dedicated love-sick admirers, namely Tim Foley and Greathouse, Lance's boss. They are true gentlemen, but they make their admiration known.

Lance is featured in another scene when, like John Spear, he rides a freshet. Lance, for the excitement of it has asked a young boatman, Stormy Nagoette, to take him along on his oil barge:

> All at once, as if by prearranged signal, quiet settled down upon the assemblage, and in the peak of it came the call.
>
> "Fresh-et!" It was a call that rose full and lusty and rich from the throat of the big man on the bank.
>
> For a space of time nothing happened.
>
> That is, if you can call nothing the split second after a gun goes off before the bullet strikes, or after a battle command is given before the troops surge forward, or after the rumble is heard in the land before the avalanche comes.

It was gentle at first. A little rocking of the boats—even the big French Creekers with their heavy oaken gunwales and the iron-bottomed ore boats dipped and bowed a little under the urging. The front boats moved out slowly—very slowly, because they received the impetus last—but the ones in the rear strained and bucked against the poles in the hands of the boatmen.

The pressure was on. Plenty of it. There was the sound of roaring water, growing in volume, growing in speed, growing in force. It hit the rear boats first, sweeping them along at a furious rate, the bigger ones riding over the smaller craft —riding them down, crushing them, and plunging on through the wreckage.

Lance wanted to close his eyes when he heard the splintering of wood and the hoarse cries of the men swept under. He wanted to, but he would not. *You wanted this, yella-belly now take it.*

He saw why Stormy Nageotte was called the best pilot on Oil Creek. The boy was laughing and singing snatches of songs as he needled and wedged his way among other craft and swung around wreckage that was turning broadside in the water.

They swept full-tilt: past meadows where horses and cattle dashed away as far as fences would allow, to wait quivering and wide-eyed for the fury to pass by; past patches of dense woods and clearings where people waved and called, their voices lost in the uproar; past houses huddled together in villages.

Following the creek, and sometimes inundated by the rushing waters, was the road where muddy, tired horses plodded as they towed the empty boats up Oil Creek for the next freshet. A teamster, mis-

> judging the hour of the freshet, had been caught in the fury of water and was clinging desperately to the roots of a huge old oak tree, his leg crumpled under him and his boat lying about him, crushed like an eggshell. The churning water washed up to his armpits, then receded-up again, receding....
>
> As Lance stared, horrified, the face was gone — a distorted mask — into the yellow flood. (KD 106-7)

Downstream from this, Stormy is killed and Lance barely escapes with his life.

Lance eventually makes enough money as a teamster to invest in a well. He becomes moderately wealthy, but he never tells Kim any thing about his business. After many adventures, fights, and scrapes, Lance is smart enough to see the end of Pit Hole and sells his interests in the well and deposits his money in Virginia. Fushia has to leave town to avoid testifying in a murder trial, so eventually and not too happily Lance and Kim plan to go back to Still Meadows to make a life together.

But not before more than half of Pit Hole burns in a three-day fire:

> The fire, newly released, raced again and flung itself crazily, burning to high heaven and racing with every breath of the wind, burning up one street and down another — stores, hotels, places of entertainment, places of business — licking almost daintily at the shacks on the hillsides which the people had built for homes, then turning back into the valley. (KD 282)

Greathouse, Lance's former boss and Kim's admirer, is wiped out in the fire and depletion of the field.

Shortly afterwards, he is blasted to bits as a load of nitroglycerin he is carrying explodes. Her other admirer, Tim Foley, the admitted killer of Cash Wilson, has broken from jail and left the area.

Tim Foley is not the only one leaving town. By late Autumn, everyone is:

> The people were going. Some loaded their wagons high with everything they owned. They were the ones who were going to oilfields in Pennsylvania: to Shamburg and Pleasantville and Oil City. They were the ones who went our of their dwellings or places of business, leaving the doors swinging idly in the summer wind and rain.
>
> Others just went away. Closed the door on everything but the few personal belongings they were carrying out. The town druggist went out this way: the people who came to his door, seeing the patent medicine staring back from the shelves, thought he had gone out to eat or to take a walk. For days they came hunting him. (KD 299)

So Kim is happy to get out of Pit Hole and back to a more settled life on the estate in Virginia.

Still another melodrama, *Kim Dawson*, published in 1950 is as over-written and melodramatic as any of the earlier works. Kim and Lance leave Pit Hole little changed after all the tumult they have been through.

The following year, 1951, an even more melodramatic novel was published, *Stoney Batter* by, Zoda Elizabeth Anderson. In it, two brothers leave home together, one is all bad, the other all good. They live as neighbors on stony farms in Western Pennsylvania during the oil exploration period. Oil and coal play a minor part in the plot.

I'll end this survey of oilfield novels of the 1940s and 50s with a brief description of another melodramatic work, *Fabulous Valley* (1956) by Cornelia Stratton Parker. The central character, Linda Rinn, like Kim Dawson, is a long suffering, honest, loving wife. She, too, is from a poor family, but she marries someone of a similar background, a hard working, dull, ignorant farmer, Silas Rinn. She soon falls in love with a handsome, sophisticated man who is attracted to her, Nathan Allen. Except for a single kiss, she remains faithful to Silas. She has one child, Davy, with Silas before he dies. She dedicates herself to raising her son alone, always hoping to see Nathan Allen again. Oil fever comes to the valley, and Linda is unhappy about the changes it brings even though they had been destitute before and now her son Davy can make a good living hauling oil.

Nothing of the oil drilling and production itself is in this book, but there are many details of how oil affects the people. Eventually, oil leasing comes to their part of the valley, and Linda, unable to write, makes her mark on a lease. They sell some of their acres for a million dollars and become extremely wealthy. Davy leaves his wife and child behind and moves to Philadelphia where he spends as wildly and unwisely as Coal Oil Johnny. Indeed, he comes to be called Rock Oil Davy. He returns home destitute. She eventually finds love with Nathan Allen. In spite of being about exciting events in an exciting time, this is a tedious and repetitious book with rather dull characters.

Like the authors of the earlier oilfield novels, the authors of the books of the forties and fifties wrote much better when describing the oilfield and what happened in it. They provided vivid descriptions of the work of the teamsters, of spring-pole drilling, of floods, of fires, of boomtown life. Once they got into love and family relations they wrote sentimentally, creating pasteboard characters, either good or bad.

Chapter 18

Golden Butterfly

It was wild and wooley there for awhile and may be again soon. Chesapeake Energy and others are rushing into the old Eastern fields in order to use in the Marcellus Shale their new expertise of horizontal drilling, developed in the Barnett Shale. There may be a new boom similar to the natural gas boom going on around Fort Worth.

But nothing will ever be like those first booms, those first discoveries in the two Petrolias, the ones in Ontario and in Western Pennsylvania, coming just after the gold rush and gold fever. They brought oil fever, the craze that hit people in those first glory days — the golden butterfly flew east.

The novelists may not have been there those first days, but they were not far behind, chronicling the transitions, the booms and busts. They were Victorians, with all of the excesses of style, of florid language, that we condemn today. I have often in the summaries and samplings from these works shown these excesses and have labeled the works melodramatic and sentimental. So they were, but I have also shown the realistic elements, the detailed description of the day-to-day work in the oilfield, the drilling for and producing of oil, the transporting of it, the pipeline building, the gauging.

These, and the fires and floods, are not exclusive to the Eastern oilfields. If readers continue to read my

Cavalcade of Oilfield Fiction, they will see these same elements in the booms to follow — from the salt dome and marshes of Spindletop to the tarpits of La Brea.

But in some ways these early novels are different from those that came later. Torpedoing has a much more important role in these first novels because Roberts' patent was in place, and there was the practice of moonshining and the resultant use of spotters. This enabled writer's like Melville Philips to introduce the macabre humor of Tickly Bender. And William Canfield could use the spotter as a villain.

The freshet plays a major role in the early novels. In no other place was such a bizarre method of moving oil used. There is more about teamsters moving oil in these novels, too. In other oilfields the teamsters mainly move machinery.

There is some use of dialect in later novels of other oilfields, but almost every author of these novels loved dialect. This can be seen by the speech of some of my favorite characters — Tickly Bender, Een Underwood, and Fighting Gib.

But what these novelists did was to give us a feel for this first home of oil fever, of being there, of being a part of the lives of people like Een and Mandy Underwood, to come to understand how some welcomed the change, others hated it, how some adjusted to it or didn't, to learn how their lives were changed quickly and changed again even more quickly

Next stop for the golden butterfly and the cavalcade — Spindletop.

Works Cited

Anderson, Zoda Elizabeth. *Stoney Batter*. Wm. B. Eerdmans Publishing Company: Grand Rapids Michigan, 1951.

Atkinson, William. *Western Stories*. Edinburgh: W & R Chambers, 1893.

Barbe, Waitman. *In the Virginias*. Akron, Ohio: 1896.

Besant, Walter and James Rice. *The Golden Butterfly*. New York: R. F. Fenno & Company, 1877.

"Birthplace of Commercial Oil in North America." The Oil Museum of Canada. 25 June 2001. <http://www.rvtravelog.com/canada.dir/canadaoil.dir/canadaoil1.htm> (22 January 2004).

Black, Brian. *Petrolia: the Landscape of America's First Oil Boom*. Baltimore: John Hopkins University Press, 2000.

Brantly, J. E. *History of Oil Well Drilling*. Houston: Gulf Publishing, 1971.

Butler, Bion H. *The Church On Quintuple Mountain*. Southern Pines, NC: Foss, Stradley & Butler, 1912.

Canfield, William W. *The Spotter A Romance of the Oil Region*. The New York: R.F. Fenno & Co. 1907.

Chernow, Ron. *Titan: The Life of John D. Rockefeller, Sr*. New York: Random House, 1998.

Daniels, Gertrude Potter. *The Warners: An American Story of Today*. Chicago: Jamieson-Higgins Co., 1901.

Eyssens, Margaret. *Go Devil*. Garden City, N. J.: Doubleday & Company, 1947.

Fox, Amy. *Kim Dawson*. Garden City, N. Y.: Doubleday &Company, 1950.

Giddens, Paul H. *Early Days of Oil: A Pictorial History of the Beginnings of the Industry in Pennsylvania*. Princeton, New Jersey: Princeton University Press, 1948.

Hager, Dorsey. *Oil Field Practice*. New York: McGraw-Hill Book Company, 1921.

Higgins, George H. and Margaret Higgins Haffey. *Tract Number 3377 A Romance of the Oil* Region. Boston: The C.M. Clark Publishing Co., 1909.

Hyne, C. J. Cutliffe. *The Wild-Catters A Tale of the Pennsylvanian Oil-Fields*. London: The Sunday School Union, 1895.

Lindstrom, E. George. *Out of the Sand*. Cleveland: High Twelve Publishing Company, 1943.

Munroe, Kirk. *Prince Dusty: A Story of the Oil Regions*. New York: G. P. Putnam's Sons, 1891.

O'Day, John Christopher. *Oil Wells in the Woods*. New York: The Oquaga Press, 1906.

Oliver, Charles H. *"646" and the Trouble Man*. Chicago: Rand McNally &Co, 1916.

Parker, Cornelia Stratton. *Fabulous Valley: A Novel of Historic Pennsylvania*. New York: G. P. Putnam's Sons, 1956.

Philips, Melville. *The Devil's Hat A Sketch in Oil*. Boston: Ticknor and Company, 1887.

Rangeler, Harry. *Silenced by Gold*, The Story of a Wildcat Well. New York: The Abbey Press, 1902.

Tarbell, Ida. *All in The Days Work: An Autobiography*. New York: The Macmillan Company, 1939.

-----. *The History of the Standard Oil Company*. New York, Macmillan Co., 1933.

Thorpe, Francis Newton. *The Divining Rod A Story of the Oil Regions*. Boston: Little, Brown, and Company, 1905.

Williamson, Harold F., Arnold R. Daum, et al. *The American Petroleum Industry: The Age of Illumination, 1859-1899*. Evanston: Northwestern University Press, 1959.

Index

Symbols

"646" 94, 127, 150, 152, 154, 155, 157, 177

A

Allegheny River 28, 32, 130, 133
All In the Day's Work 30
The American Medical Oil Company 18
anchor 49
Samuel Andrews 73, 74
John Archbold 77
W. B. Atkinson 58

B

Waitman Barbe 61, 63
Walter Besant 21
George Bissell 18
Brian Black 28
Blaney farm 127
Bradford 78, 93, 94, 97
Francis Brewer 19
Burkeville, Kentucky 18
Bion Butler 121

C

J. N. Camden 78
Canada 21, 26, 176
William Canfield 101
Charleston, West Virginia 17
Charlie Ransom 58, 61
Chernow 73, 84, 100, 101, 176
Cherry Grove 65
Cherry Run 30
The Church On Quintuple Mountain 121
Maurice Clark 73
Columbia Conduit Company 79

connection gang 132
Cumberland River 18

D

dance hall 130
Gertrude Potter Daniels 82
C. A. Dean 73
Alphonse de Rothschild 80
The Devil's Hat: A Sketch in Oil (1887) 35
Divining Rod 89, 178
Edwin L. Drake 19

E

Empire Oil 78
engineer 131, 132, 139

F

first refiner 18
Henry Flagler 74

G

gambler 121, 124, 125
gauging 127, 157
gusher 35, 37, 40

H

Margaret Haffey 106
George H. Higgins 106

I

"In the Virginias" 61
Imperial Refining Company 77

K

kerosene 73, 74, 80, 81, 91
Samuel Kier 18
Thomas Kier 18

L

leases 67
lightning 133, 134
E. George Lindstrom 158, 159

M

"mystery" well 37, 114
market 32, 40, 43
McElhenny Farm 31
McKean County 94
moonshiner 37, 46, 48, 104
moonshining 44, 104
Kirk Munroe, 48

N

Nelly 94
New York Central 75
nitroglycerin 37, 41, 48, 50, 54 58, 87, 104, 105
Robert Nobel 80

O

O'Day 93, 98, 100, 177
John Christopher O'Day 93
oil-fever 37
Oil City 36, 39, 40, 76, 77, 95, 97, 158
Oil City *Derrick* 158, 159
Oil Creek 19, 28, 31
Oil Creek Tales 158
Oil Exchange 71, 124
oil producer 130, 152
Oil Springs, Ontario 21, 25
Oil Well In the Woods 93
Ontario 21, 22, 25
Out of the Sand 158

P

The Pennsylvania Railroad 78
Petrolia 28, 31, 176
Melville Philips 35

Pit Hole 32, 35 93
Prince Dusty 48, 55, 56

R

railroads 134
Harry Rangeler 85
refineries 28, 33, 132
James Rice 21
Colonel E. A. L. Roberts 37
Rockefeller 73, 74, 75, 76, 77, 78, 79, 81, 84, 100, 101, 176
Henry Rouse 30
roustabouts 131
David Ruffner 17, 18

S

the saloon keeper 124
Marcus Samuel 80
Tom Scott 79
scouts 36, 66
Seneca oil 18
Hugh Nixon Shaw 21
Silenced by Gold 85, 178
Smith, Uncle Billy 19
William A., "Uncle Billy," Smith 19
The Spotter 176
Standard 73, 74, 76, 77, 78, 79, 80, 81, 82, 89, 93, 97, 98, 99, 100, 101, 126, 127 178
steamboats 32
surveyor 70, 71

T

Ida Tarbell 30
Tarentum, Pennsylvania 18
Tarr farm 32
telegraph 127, 132, 135, 136, 138, 140, 142, 148, 149, 150,
The Devil's Hat 35, 37, 47, 177
The Golden Butterfly 21, 176
Francis Newton Thorpe 89

Tidewater Pipeline 79
Tidioute 45
Titusville 19, 28, 36
Tomhicken 60
tool dresser 85, 87, 124, 128, 129, 130, 140
James Townsend 19
Tract Number 3377 106, 177
train 134, 135
Triumph Hill 94

V

Samuel Van Syckle 32

W

The Warners 82, 176
Western Stories 58
The Wild-Catters: 65
wildcat 37, 43, 65, 66, 129, 145, 150

www.ingramcontent.com/pod-product-compliance
Lightning Source LLC
Chambersburg PA
CBHW051756040426
42446CB00007B/391